MOUNTAIN WALKS
YORKSHIRE THREE PEAKS

MOUNTAIN WALKS
YORKSHIRE THREE PEAKS

15 ROUTES TO ENJOY ON AND AROUND PEN-Y-GHENT, INGLEBOROUGH AND WHERNSIDE

First published in 2024 by Vertebrate Publishing.

Vertebrate Publishing
Omega Court, 352 Cemetery Road, Sheffield S11 8FT, United Kingdom.
www.adventurebooks.com

Copyright © 2024 Hannah Collingridge and Vertebrate Publishing Ltd.

Hannah Collingridge has asserted her rights under the Copyright, Designs and Patents Act 1988 to be identified as author of this work.

A CIP catalogue record for this book is available from the British Library.

ISBN 978-1-83981-224-8 (Paperback)
ISBN 978-1-83981-225-5 (Ebook)

All rights reserved. No part of this work covered by the copyright herein may be reproduced or used in any form or by any means – graphic, electronic, or mechanised, including photocopying, recording, taping, or information storage and retrieval systems – without the written permission of the publisher.

Front cover: Ingleborough from White Scars above Crina Bottom.
Back cover: Pen-y-ghent from near Jubilee Cave above Settle.
Photography by Joolze Dymond unless otherwise credited.
www.joolzedymond.com

All maps reproduced by permission of Ordnance Survey on behalf of The Controller of His Majesty's Stationery Office. © Crown Copyright. AC0000809882

Design and production by Jane Beagley
www.adventurebooks.com

Printed and bound in Bulgaria by Pulsio.

Vertebrate Publishing is committed to printing on paper from sustainable sources.

FSC MIX Paper from responsible sources FSC® C128169

Every effort has been made to achieve accuracy of the information in this guidebook. The authors, publishers and copyright owners can take no responsibility for: loss or injury (including fatal) to persons; loss or damage to property or equipment; trespass, irresponsible behaviour or any other mishap that may be suffered as a result of following the route descriptions or advice offered in this guidebook. The inclusion of a track or path as part of a route, or otherwise recommended, in this guidebook does not guarantee that the track or path will remain a right of way. If conflict with landowners arises we advise that you act politely and leave by the shortest route available. If the matter needs to be taken further then please take it up with the relevant authority.

MOUNTAIN WALKS
YORKSHIRE THREE PEAKS

15 ROUTES TO ENJOY ON AND AROUND PEN-Y-GHENT, INGLEBOROUGH AND WHERNSIDE

HANNAH COLLINGRIDGE

Vertebrate Publishing, Sheffield
www.adventurebooks.com

Contains Ordnance Survey Data © Crown Copyright and Database Right.

Download the Mountain Walks Yorkshire Three Peaks GPX files from
www.adventurebooks.com/MWY3P-GPX

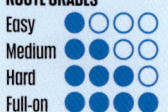

ROUTE GRADES
Easy ●○○○
Medium ●●○○
Hard ●●●○
Full-on ●●●●

/ CONTENTS

Introduction ... vii
Acknowledgements ... viii
About the walks ... viii
Navigation ... ix
Safety & well-being ... x
Weather ... xi
Kit & comfort ... xii
Fuelling & nutrition ... xiii
Mountain rescue ... xv
Behaviour & respecting the environment ... xv
Walking with your dog ... xvii
How to use this book ... xviii
Rocks & place names ... xviii

THE ROUTES

/ 01 Ingleborough Estate Nature Trail from Clapham ●○○○ 4.8km/3 miles ... 1
/ 02 Around Ribblehead ●○○○ 6.2km/3.9 miles ... 5
/ 03 Stainforth Scar & the lime kilns ●●○○ 5km/3.1 miles ... 9
/ 04 Settle to Attermire Scar & Victoria Cave ●●○○ 7.1km/4.4 miles ... 15
/ 05 Stainforth & Feizor ●●○○ 10.2km/6.3 miles ... 21
/ 06 Yordas Cave & Turbary Road ●●○○ 11.5km/7.1 miles ... 29
/ 07 Pen-y-ghent from Horton in Ribblesdale ●●○○ 10.2km/6.3 miles ... 35
/ 08 Pen-y-ghent & Plover Hill ●●○○ 13.6km/8.5 miles ... 41
/ 09 Ingleborough from Clapham ●●●○ 16.6km/10.3 miles ... 47
/ 10 Ingleborough from Ingleton ●●●○ 14.3km/8.9 miles ... 53
/ 11 Whernside from Ribblehead ●●●○ 12.7km/7.9 miles ... 59
/ 12 Whernside from Dent ●●●○ 19.3km/12 miles ... 65
/   All Three Peaks in One ... 73
/ 13 Yorkshire Three Peaks: anticlockwise ●●●● 39.4km/24.5 miles ... 75
/ 14 Yorkshire Three Peaks: clockwise ●●●● 39.4km/24.5 miles ... 86
/   Yorkshire Three Peaks: multi-day itineraries ... 92
/ 15 Super Three Peaks ●●●● 47km/29.2 miles ... 95

Appendix ... 110

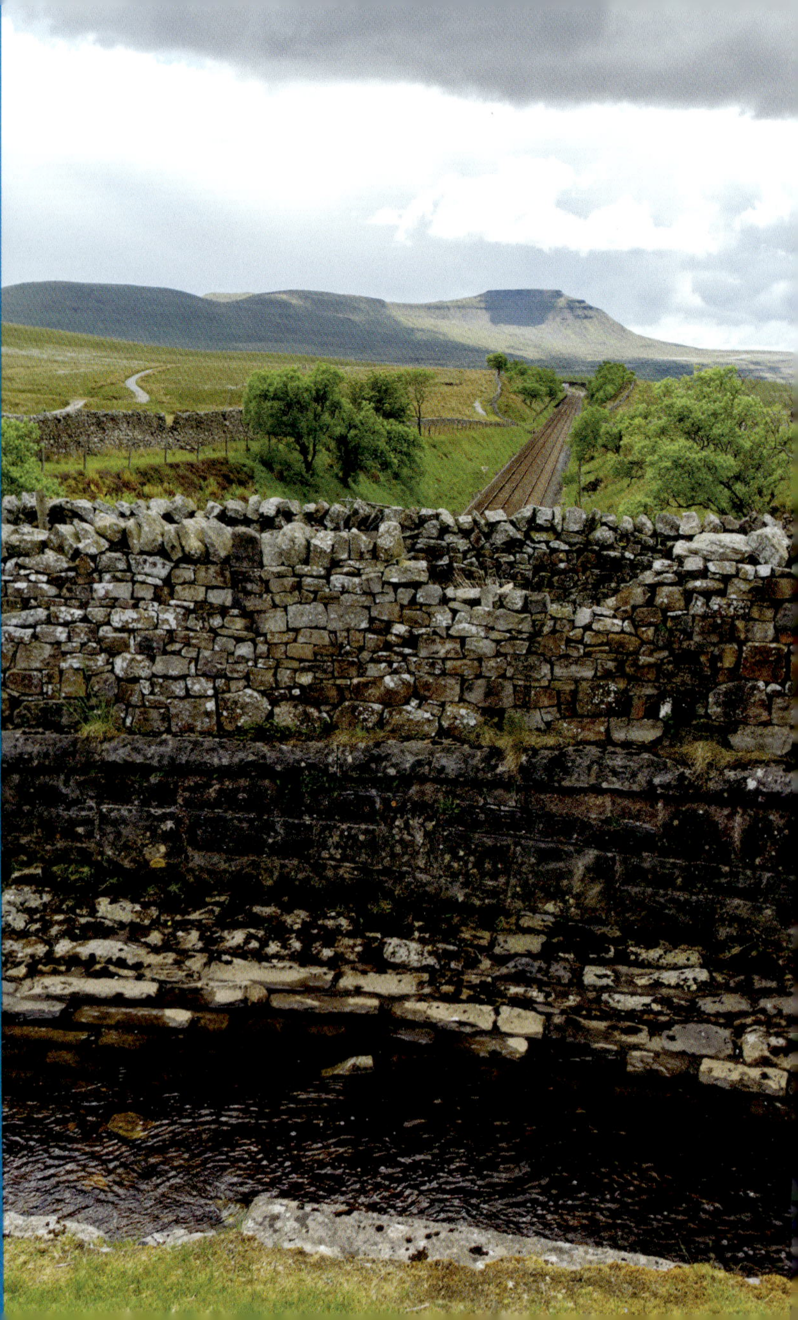

/ INTRODUCTION

Pen-y-ghent, Ingleborough and Whernside – commonly known as the Three Peaks – sit within the Yorkshire Dales National Park, designated as such in 1954, but they only cover a tiny part of the park as a whole. It's a very special and splendid part, along the south-western boundary and just north of the Forest of Bowland, noted for its particular geology which gives the landscape its distinctive feel.

It's really the limestone that makes it quite so special. Whereas in other areas the limestone is well buried, faulting and geological shifts have brought it to the surface here. The bedrock south of Ingleton, for instance, is older than the gritstone capping on the top of Ingleborough which is 600 metres higher but only five kilometres away. To the base limestone and the Yoredale Group of banded sandstones, shales and limestone above it, add the sculpting power of water and ice. That gives us the limestone pavements, the distinctive stepped shape of the hills and a whole separate landscape beneath the surface. Glimpses and the odd foray into that underground world are possible even by those who have no desire for caving or potholing. There have been show caves in the area since at least the Victorian period, and both White Scar and Ingleborough show caves allow safe and easy access to the subterranean landscape. There are also a couple of free options if you take a good torch on your walks.

There have been people living and working here since the last retreat of ice over 10,000 years ago, and evidence for animals long before that – the oldest bones found in Victoria Cave are 130,000 years old. There are traces of prehistoric settlements, along with evidence of Romano-British-era settlements and travel. The Welsh, Old English and Old Norse place names describe how the area was farmed and lived on. There are clearings, shielings, shelters, pastures, boggy bits to be avoided, places to acquire useful materials; everything for living. Later, the great monastic houses left their marks, particularly notable for us are their trade routes. And, of course, the Settle–Carlisle Railway is always present in the area, especially distinctive at Ribblehead with the great Batty Moss viaduct. It's interesting to muse what would have changed if the line had been shut in the 1980s as planned.

It's a breathtakingly beautiful area that is worth exploring in detail, even underground. These walks, from the short and accessible through to the challenge of the full Three Peaks, are designed to help you discover why this is such a special and justifiably popular part of the country.

Hannah Collingridge

Ingleborough from the aqueduct over the Settle–Carlisle line. © John Coefield

ACKNOWLEDGEMENTS

Authors do not write books without immense help and support. In this case, my thanks go to my parents who first introduced me to the area, my mum with whom I did so much of my early walking, and my wife who is ever supportive and runs the bath when I get back battered from trips. As ever, photo thanks to Joolze Dymond who sees what I cannot; Alpkit have been brilliant at helping me with gear; Rosie Montgomery of *@rosieknits_* made me The Best Ever woolly hats and gloves for the hills; Matt and Marcus of Torq Fitness have been invaluable in helping advise on the nutrition and fuelling necessary for endurance – the ***www.torqfitness.co.uk*** website has a wealth of info about fuelling; Matt from Run and Ride in Staffordshire recommended shoes and rolled his eyes at my sock preferences; Tim, Ben and Donna of Schwalbe Tyres have been slightly less useful than usual but that's the nature of walking rather than cycling guides; Kate Hilditch from YDNP answered all my questions patiently and accurately; fellow female writing buddies Lina Arthur and Kerri Andrews understand so much about this process. To all those friends who provide support and silliness when required, much love. And thank you to the Vertebrate team for banter, books, brilliance and belief.

ABOUT THE WALKS

Most of the land in the Yorkshire Dales is privately owned and most of the upland areas are farmed one way or another. There are miles of historical public rights of way in the form of public footpaths and bridleways across the area, some having been used for hundreds if not thousands of years. There is also 'access land' marked on maps, arising from the Countryside and Rights of Way Act 2000 (CRoW Act, sometimes referred to as the 'right to roam'). For clarity, ease of use and planning, the walks described in this guidebook usually follow established public rights of way, where you have the legal right to 'pass and repass' along the way. Sections of walks in upland terrain follow established paths over CRoW access land and some of these routes are clearer than others on the ground, depending on the popularity of the area. Some routes over access land are mapped and some are not; this may also depend on what type of mapping you're using.

The timings quoted for each walk are quite generous, assuming an average walking pace of 3–4km/h (2–3mph), which also factors in time for breaks, photos and the effort of ascent/terrain as applicable. If you are likely to get completely sidetracked poking at something interesting along the way, add more time. The 'running' times quoted reflect the fact that a runner may move more efficiently over most terrain, but will still walk many of the ascents, moving at an average speed of 5–8km/h (3–5mph).

/ NAVIGATION

The mapping and descriptions in this guidebook are intended for planning and information; you will need to use additional mapping and navigation methods while walking, either a hard-copy map and compass, or good quality online mapping app (such as OS Maps, Gaia GPS, OutdoorActive or Topo GPS) on a mobile phone or GPS unit. Both require practice; understanding maps and symbols and orienting yourself from them is a useful skill to learn; there are many tutorial videos online that can help with this.

While many mountain users access route and mapping information on mobile devices or GPS units, be aware that digital mapping sources can drain your mobile phone/GPS unit's battery; make sure that you carry a hard-copy map which does not rely on having mobile phone signal and will increase your ability to see the bigger picture. Pack a portable power bank to recharge your device on the hill, especially if you also want to use your phone to make calls or take photos.

Generally speaking, navigation in good weather around the route of the Three Peaks is pretty straightforward; there is good signposting and clear, well-maintained paths. Plus, it's likely that others will be doing the same route on the same day so there will be people to ask or follow. However, in weather that isn't so good, things can become much more tricky: the summit of Ingleborough is a particularly well-known spot for navigational errors in mist, especially when you are tired. It is good practice to take a map and compass with you; it's even better practice to know how to use them. Even the basic compass function of finding which way is north can be immensely helpful.

Navigation through farmland where footpaths cross several walls can be surprisingly difficult. Knowing which side of a wall your footpath is supposed to be on can be an immense help and potentially save you from the wrath of landowners. Many things are signposted, but signposts suffer from weathering and being used as scratching posts by livestock. Don't expect there to be a signpost or waymarker at every single path junction.

There are many great things about modern technology, including navigation on GPS and smartphones. These are not infallible but Mountaineering Scotland (***www.mountaineering.scot***) have produced some handy guidelines about their use:

1 **CHARGE** – start with 100 per cent battery charge, and charge your device while you travel if you're using it for music or road navigation.
2 **PROTECT** – protect your phone from the elements and keep it close to your body when not in use to help it stay warm and dry and save battery life. Sealable freezer bags are incredibly handy.
3 **DOWNLOAD** – download all the maps you need; don't rely on mobile data to access them. Include maps of surrounding areas (in case you need to change

your route) and use a topographic map (like OS or Harvey Maps) – not all digital maps are suitable for hiking in the hills. (I personally love having a map on my phone screen mainly because you can zoom in on detail easily without finding another pair of glasses.)

4 **EXTEND** – switching your phone to 'flight mode' makes your battery last a lot longer. Take a fully charged power bank (and cable) to recharge on the go if needed. If you are using the phone for photos as well it's well worth switching to flight mode.

5 **TAKE A BACKUP** – if your phone or GPS fails, you'll need another way to navigate, for example a map and compass, and the ability to use them effectively. Consider also carrying a simple backup phone for emergencies.

If you are unsure of your navigational skills, there are plenty of books, videos and courses available. Make sure you can rely on your own skills to get out of trouble rather than others or clever gadgets.

The walks in this book appear on the following map:

- **Ordnance Survey OL2 Yorkshire Dales: Southern & Western areas – 1:25,000**

… with the exception of Stainforth & Feizor (walk 5), which is on **Ordnance Survey OL41 Forest of Bowland & Ribblesdale (1:25,000)** as well. Frustrating.

Harvey Maps also do a Mountain Map (1:40,000) of the Yorkshire Dales, which just about covers most of the walks in this book.

/ SAFETY & WELL-BEING

Keeping safe and well in upland terrain starts with an appropriate plan that suits both you and your group and the forecast weather and mountain conditions, and allows for enjoyment and adventure along the way. Bear in mind that a robust plan will allow for changes; you shouldn't be locked into a single objective, as outside factors may influence your day. These factors might include changeable weather and how it affects you on the hill, how you/the group are feeling given the terrain or effort, your estimated/actual speed of travel, the length of daylight hours, parking and access/public transport times, what clothing you're wearing/carrying and even how much food/drink you have with you. Let someone outside your group know where you're going and what time you're expecting to be back down (and let them know when you're off the hill to prevent them from worrying). When planning your day, check out ***www.adventuresmart.uk*** for helpful tips and reminders of what factors to consider. #BeAdventureSmart

First, have a plan which considers the abilities and speed of your group: how long is the walk, how much ascent is there, what is the terrain like? Also consider the forecast weather and amount of light in the day: have you enough time to do the

Ribblehead (Batty Moss) viaduct. © John Coefield

walk in daylight, are you prepared for walking after sunset, how windy and wet is it likely to be, or, more rarely, are you prepared for sun and heat?

Then, be prepared to adapt that plan as things change. For example, weather systems might be moving at a different speed to what was forecasted – very common in British upland areas; how you and your group are feeling – some days you're the pigeon, some days the statue; how fast the group is moving – sometimes a minor injury may make it sensible to cut the walk short. Let someone know where you are going and also what time to call Mountain Rescue if they haven't heard you are back safely. If you do a lot of solo walking, a tracker can act as a reassuring backup.

|WEATHER

The Met Office (***www.metoffice.gov.uk***) provides separate forecasts for the summits of all three peaks, as well as the surrounding towns. This is useful as they give the wind speeds and temperatures at hilltop level rather than valley level, which gives a better indication of walking conditions. The Mountain Weather Information Service (MWIS – ***www.mwis.org.uk***) also provides a hill forecast for the Yorkshire Dales and North Pennines, including the Three Peaks area, with information about precipitation, wind chill, visibility, the chance of cloud-free summits and how cold it is likely to be at height.

Why are these of interest?
Wind: wind speeds can have a huge effect on temperature and on ease of walking. Walking in high or buffeting winds is not easy and can be tiring, especially if you have a long walk planned. Wind can also add far too much excitement when on an exposed ridge.

Wind chill: this is literally the chilling effect of the wind on the temperature but also on you. Emerging from a sheltered climb, maybe damp from exertion, into a windier area can mean your temperature drops rapidly. If you can hear it's windy above you, stop and put your coat on before coming out of the sheltered area.

Visibility: how far you can see. On good days this may just affect how good the view is or if it's a bit blurry. On days when the clag is down, it can sometimes mean you can barely see your hand in front of you, and if your navigation isn't up to scratch it can all go horribly wrong (see page ix).

Temperature: if it's lovely and warm at valley level, it's tempting to think it will remain so for your whole walk. It may do. It's more likely there are going to be temperature changes – as a rule of thumb you lose 1 °C for every 100 metres ascended in dry air – so extra layers are always worth taking. Plus, it's not about having the gear for when a walk goes smoothly; it's about being able to look after yourself and your group when things go wrong. If an injury were to cause your party to stop on the hillside, would you have the clothing to keep warm until the situation was resolved? Stick an extra layer in your bag.

In short, consider the weather conditions carefully. Don't feel you have to stick to the original plan. Picking a lower-level walk or cutting a longer walk short are all better options on days when the weather is not what you wished for. Some folk thrive in battling the elements, others call that a cafe day.

/ KIT & COMFORT

Let's talk layers and materials. First, avoid cotton which loses insulating properties when damp with sweat or wet with rain and take ages to dry out. Synthetic or natural fabrics such as bamboo and wool are a better option. In warm, sunny weather remember to protect your arms, head and neck, as well as slapping on your sunscreen – use a high-factor screen, preferably a sporty one that is sweat resistant.

Comfortable, synthetic walking trousers or leggings are a good option, as is a synthetic top or base layer over which warm layers can be added. Take a rucksack containing an extra warm layer (or two if it's very cold), a pair of warm gloves and a hat, a zippable, waterproof jacket with a large hood, and waterproof trousers that you can pull over your walking trousers/leggings. Layering several thinner layers is more flexible than wearing a very thick ski jacket or similar. Your rucksack should also contain food, drink, a map, a phone charger and power bank, and a waterproof bag or bags to keep everything in. You might also wish to include a head torch (and spare batteries), depending on the time of year/time of day that you're planning to walk, a small first aid kit, and an emergency group shelter that you can sit on or in for lunch breaks or use for emergency shelter in the event of an unforeseen situation or injury.

Footwear: for the full route it's crucial you are comfortable and confident moving over potentially tricky terrain in whatever you are wearing. Now is not the time to try something new. Because the full Three Peaks route paths are so well-maintained, an off-road trainer (not flat soled) might well be sufficient, or you may prefer a boot for more ankle support and waterproofing. A full-on mountain boot with a stiff sole isn't necessary here. For some of the other walks, especially after rain, a boot and gaiter combo is preferable unless you are used to and happy walking with wet feet.

Ticks can carry Lyme disease; they lurk in the bracken and long vegetation in summer so walking trousers are advised during this season. Walk in the middle of paths and avoid unnecessarily walking through bushy vegetation or long grass. Advice for preventing tick bites and tick removal is available here: **www.lymediseaseaction.org.uk**

Check a mountain weather forecast to ensure that you pack the kit you need (including precautionary extras) and make sure you wear a watch so you can keep track of time. Always 'Stop and Be Bothered' to change/add a layer rather than ignoring what your body or the weather is telling you.

/ FUELLING & NUTRITION

Do not underestimate how much energy you will need for a big walk. Let us say you are going to be out for 12 hours on the full Three Peaks route. The intensity of your effort will generally be quite low with occasional periods of higher intensity on the ascents. First, pace yourself. Aim for a steady plod that you can keep up for a good length of time. If you can hold a conversation with someone, even yourself, then it's a good pace you can sustain. Dashing ahead and then having to rest isn't an efficient use of energy and will lead to fatigue. Using walking poles may help you achieve a more even pace.

Secondly, fuel. Have a good, carb-rich, meal the night before and a good breakfast before you start. Your main source of energy needs to be carbohydrate during the walk. Fat is not required – not only do you have enough fat stores on your body, whatever size you are, for fuel, but eating fatty foods will slow down digestion in your gut and therefore delay energy reaching the bits of your body you'd like it to reach. Eat little and often – aim for something every 30 to 40 minutes. Trail mix, bars, gels – all of these are handy for constant nibbling. Have a proper break and a sit down every so often – this is a great psychological boost as well. Again, keep your bigger meals carb and protein rich. If you feel you are flagging or notice someone in your group struggling, have something to eat. I like a gel and a flapjack in these cases – instant energy to boost me, and then some

Running through Sulber Nick, Pen-y-ghent ahead. © Stephen Ross

slower-burning stuff to sustain. It can be a great, instant pick-me-up. After the walk, try and eat something to help with recovery soon after you have finished. You are likely to want a bigger meal by now – this is a perfect opportunity to consume larger quantities of carbohydrate and protein to help you refuel and repair after a long, energy-demanding day.

Hydration is also incredibly important, plus it can be used as an extra way of fuelling too, especially in hot weather when it's more difficult to eat solid fuel. Ultrarunners use the trick of fuelling with fluid on the ups, and then more solid stuff on the downs and flat when their body isn't under as much stress. I tend to carry two bottles – one with plain water and one with electrolytes and energy in it – and use a water filter to top up from the streams en route. This also has the advantage of meaning I'm never carrying more than a kilogram of fluid at any one time. Water is important but it is heavy. Again, aim for little and often when drinking. If you are going to use liquid fuel, make sure you have tried it out beforehand and that it agrees with your gut.

Don't automatically plan your breaks for the tops of the hills. You may need the fuel for the up. It's often windy on top, too, and while there are shelters on top of all three peaks, they are often busy. Instead drop down the hill a way and find some shelter. Careful and constant fuelling will be a huge help on your big day out.

/ MOUNTAIN RESCUE

Mountain Rescue England and Wales is a charity that relies on volunteer time, donations and fundraising to operate. The walks in this guidebook are covered by the Cave Rescue Organisation (***www.cro.org.uk***) who handle both overground and underground rescues.

Many mountain rescue calls are made when people find themselves in exposed conditions in poor weather or darkness, lost or overcome by fatigue or cold/wet/hot weather. Making appropriate plans and amending them if needed, as well as eating adequate food and taking enough kit, clothing and mapping will help to safeguard against things unravelling during the day. That said, mountain rescue teams advise that you should always call if you need assistance. They can sometimes provide advice over the telephone to help you take the best action on the hill for you and your group.

What to do in an emergency

If you or someone else is in need of emergency assistance in the mountains, dial **999** (or **112**) and ask for **POLICE** and then **MOUNTAIN RESCUE**. This relies on you having mobile phone signal and a charged phone battery, and being able to give the relevant details over the phone when asked (location, name/s and details of people affected, what has happened and your contact details). You may be asked to stay in position or in signal range so the mountain rescue team can call you back. Keep yourself and others warm and insulated from the ground and the weather. Put on layers, eat something for energy and sit out of the wind on a bag or clothing.

Emergency rescue by SMS text

In the UK you can contact the emergency services by SMS text. While this service is primarily intended for those with hearing or speech difficulties, it can be useful if you have low battery or intermittent signal. You need to register your phone beforehand by texting '**register**' to **999** and then following the instructions in the reply. ***www.emergencysms.net***

/ BEHAVIOUR & RESPECTING THE ENVIRONMENT

Probably the thing we are all hoping for when we head to the Three Peaks is a good day out, whatever that means to each of us. And there are certain things we can do to help make sure everyone has a good day out, including those who live and work in the national park. A bit of awareness, consideration and respect go a long way.

We are incredibly lucky to have the national parks as our playgrounds, and while they are not perfect by any means, they are a great resource we can all help to cherish. There are some very simple steps you can take while on your day out.

1. **Have fun.** Appreciate your day out, the fresh air, the trails beneath your feet, the rocks, the flowers, birds, whatever you find interesting; take a moment to find some pleasure in it. Go somewhere new, visit an old favourite. Have a solo adventure or a great day out with friends.
2. **Leave no trace.** Take your rubbish back home with you – if you brought it in, take it away. Take a bag to put your wrappers in. Remember fruit skins such as satsumas and bananas take a long time to degrade in the British environment so take them home. And if you can, pick up some rubbish while you are at it – leave a positive trace.
3. **Park considerately.** Yes, it's difficult and the Dales get incredibly busy, but please park with respect. Aim to park in the designated car parks, but if you can't, try to avoid causing problems for those working, so keep gateways clear and try not to cause access issues.
4. **Be considerate.** You've planned, you've trained, the big day is here and you are super excited. Brilliant. Have a great day. However, for those living locally it's not exciting and they'd rather have a lie-in without the noise of Three Peakers invading their bedroom. So, keep the noise down around the houses, shut your car doors quietly and as little as possible, walk through the villages without too much excited chatter, and celebrate in on old-school way – think polite clapping at a cricket match in the 1950s. Not only will the locals love you for it, they won't threaten to disembowel you with a teaspoon. Everybody wins.

Any problems can be ameliorated by modifying your behaviour and attitudes in the light of the surrounding communities and landscape. For further information, see ***www.yorkshiredales.org.uk/things-to-do/get-outdoors/where-can-i-go/countryside-code***

A summary of the Countryside Code is below:

Respect everyone
- be considerate to those living in, working in and enjoying the countryside
- leave gates and property as you find them
- do not block access to gateways or driveways when parking
- be nice, say hello, share the space
- follow local signs and keep to marked paths unless wider access is available

Protect the environment
- take your litter home – leave no trace of your visit (including fruit peel, sanitary items, nappies, dog poo bags, tissue paper)
- do not light fires and only have BBQs where signs say you can
- always keep your dogs under control and in sight
- dog poo – bag it and bin it in any public waste bin or take it home
- care for nature – do not cause damage or disturbance (do not move stones, damage ruins or plants and trees, or disturb wildlife)

Enjoy the outdoors
- check your route (make sure you have the relevant maps) and local conditions
- plan your adventure – know what to expect and what you can do
- enjoy your visit, have fun, make a memory

Know the signs and symbols of the countryside
- Public Footpath, Public Bridleway
- Restricted Byway, Byway Open to All Traffic, Permissive Path
- Open Access Land, End of Open Access Land

/ WALKING WITH YOUR DOG

Shared adventures with our canine companions can be wonderful. However, given the delicate balance between outdoor recreation and farming on and around the Three Peaks, it's essential to know how to look after our dogs, both for their health and safety and for the well-being of other people and animals around us, including grazing livestock and local wildlife.

Legally, on a Public Right of Way an owner does not have to keep a dog on a lead, as long as the dog remains under 'close control'. However, the advice from Yorkshire Dales National Park is to keep dogs on a short lead. On Open Access Land, there is a legal requirement to keep dogs on a short lead between 1 March and 31 July to safeguard breeding ground-nesting birds and livestock, and owners must always be in control of their dog. On grouse moors dogs may be banned at certain times of the year – this affects Whernside from Dent (walk 12) in this book. Farmers have the legal right to destroy any dog that is causing worry or harm to livestock.

Dog poo needs to be bagged up and disposed of in an appropriate bin as it can contain bacteria and parasites which are a health risk to grazing animals, people and dogs.

Be wary of how your dog will behave around livestock. Keep your distance from cows and horses where possible, especially if the animals have their young with them. If animals closely follow or chase you, let go of your dog's lead and focus on your own safety.

/ HOW TO USE THIS BOOK

Use this book for inspiration, to improve your knowledge, find out local information and as part of your planning process. The maps in this book are the same as the Ordnance Survey Explorer OL2 and OL41 maps described on page x, but you should always take a separate map out with you in case you need to refer to the wider area around the walk. The text descriptions allow you to work your way through the route visually with a map before you set out, as well as providing a reference when you're walking. Familiarise yourself with the symbols used on the map and consider possible escape routes in case you need to retrace your steps or lose height to escape poor weather.

The descriptions of the routes in the Mountains Walks series as

Easy ●○○○
Medium ●●○○
Hard ●●●○
Full-on ●●●●

… do not just relate to the distance of the route. The gradings have been reached by considering a mixture of distance, ascent profile, type of terrain and technicality and how easy the route might be to navigate in poor weather.

Follow the advice above about choosing equipment, using mountain-specific weather forecasts and how to look after yourself and your party to maximise your enjoyment and safety. Additional information can be found via the websites listed, which offer further opportunities to increase your knowledge and confidence in planning and enjoying walks in the Three Peaks.

Map Key

S — Route starting point

2 — Route marker

↗ — Direction arrow

52 — Additional grid line numbers to aid navigation

/ ROCKS & PLACE NAMES

Let's talk layers again, but this time layers of rocks. Walking up any of the Three Peaks will involve passing through changing layers of rock types as you ascend.

Very simply put, and with apologies to all geologists, a fault line runs along the A65, making the terrain of the Three Peaks area very different to the Craven Valley. This means the Three Peaks have a great bed of limestone as their bottom layer and then above that there are thinner beds of sandstones, shales and limestones known as the Yoredale Group. All three types of rock react differently to weathering and water. Shale erodes very quickly, sandstone is impermeable and so is where the streams run on the surface, and limestone rarely has surface water but instead an underground water system of incredible magnitude. The whole area was glaciated in the last ice age, leaving wide, U-shaped valleys, limestone that has been scraped clean of everything, and the famous Ribblehead drumlin field. Drumlins are the slightly mysterious but remarkably steep-sided mounds of glacial dump that you'll come across on the link between Tarn Bar and Ribblehead in particular. Some of the most striking features are mentioned in the walks.

Then there are the place names of the Dales which give us a little insight into the people who have lived here. First, there are the three peaks themselves.

Ingleborough: the *Ingle* is probably Old English *ing* – 'peak', plus *hyll* – referring to the distinctive shape of Ingleborough, dominant in the landscape. The *borough* part comes from *burh* referring to the fort remains on top which must have been clearly visible to the locals and identifiable as a defensive feature. Ingleton is therefore the 'settlement besides *Ingle*'.

Whernside: *quern* – 'millstone', plus *side* – 'hillside', thus 'hillside where millstones are found'. The upper part of the hill is noted for its supply of useful Millstone Grit. It's interesting to consider that the name of a specific area of the hill has spread to include the whole. Though poor old Whernside has never been recognised as a particularly distinctive hill.

Pen-y-ghent: the *pen* is easily enough explained as (Primitive) Welsh – 'head, end, top, height, hill', which is found as a name through many hilly areas including nearby Pendle Hill. However, the rest of the name is not so clear and could refer to a name or an (as yet) unidentifiable element. It has been suggested it's 'hill of the wind', but there isn't any definitive evidence for that, or 'hill or the border'. It is notable though that Pen-y-ghent isn't an English name and so pre-dates the Anglo-Saxon settlers to the area. That's a whole other topic.

The Scandinavian settlers have left a distinct layer to the names, too. *Dale* (valley), *beck* (stream) and *birk* (birch) are all Norse rather than English.

Topographical names give hints and clues about the former use of the landscape: *sleights*, for instance, refers to 'level fields', important to note in an upland area; *scales* are shielings, shelters for seasonal pasturing of animals. *Clapham* is the 'homestead on the noisy stream'. It's a fascinating topic – and one for another book!

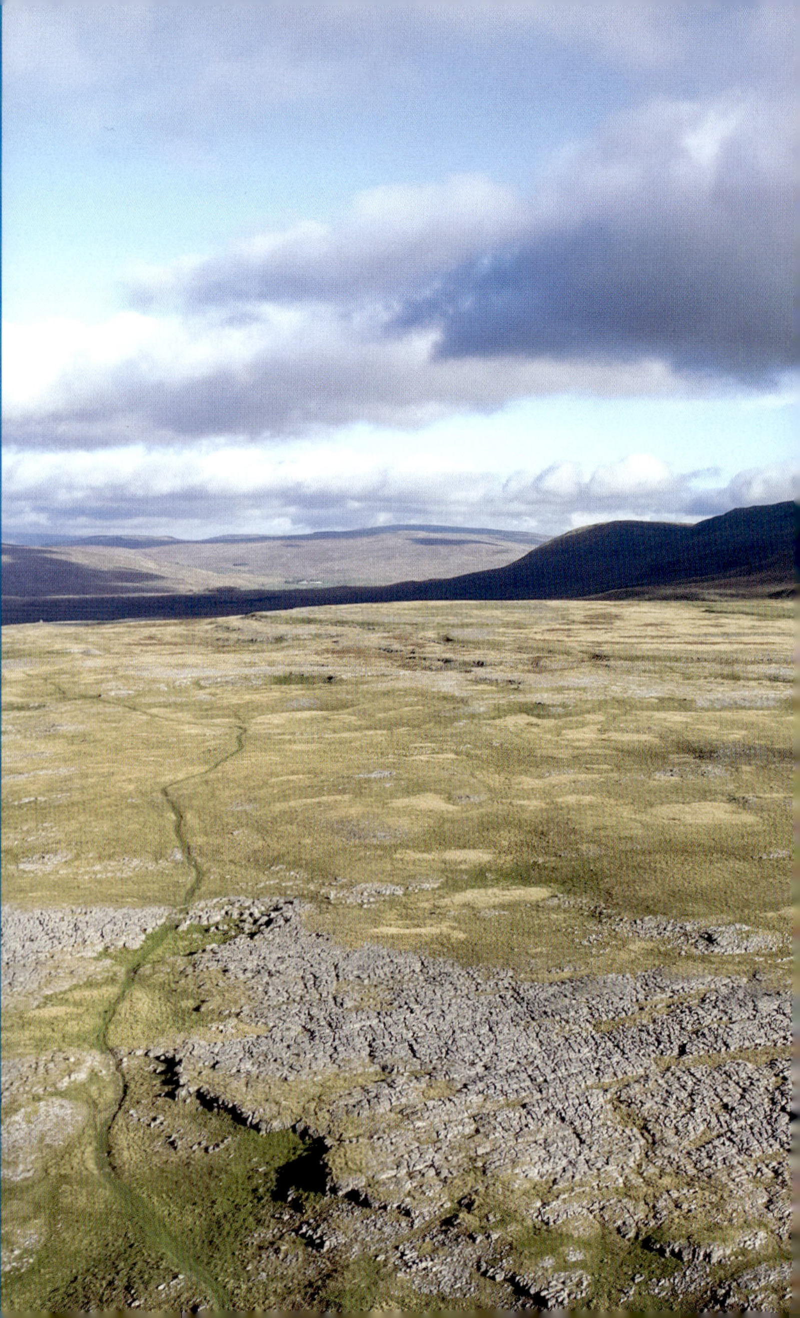

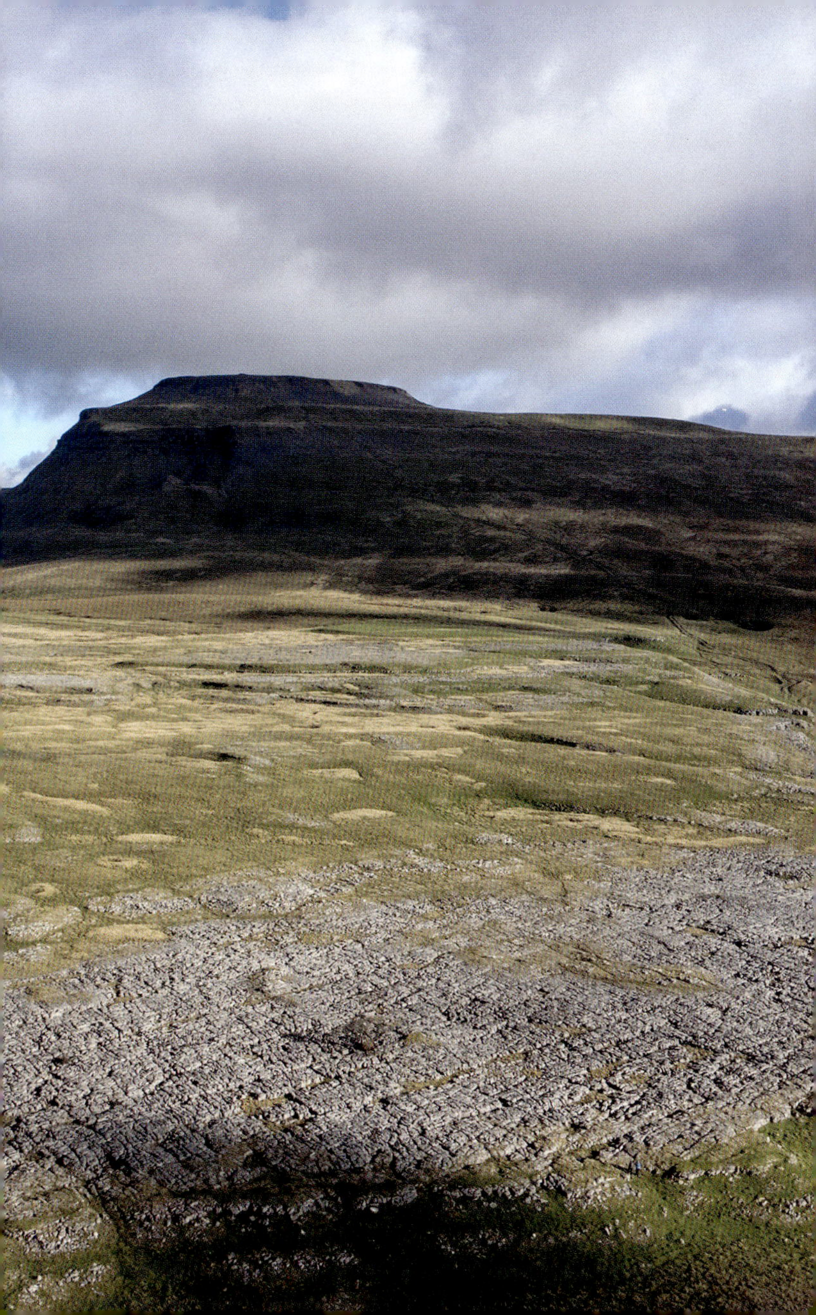

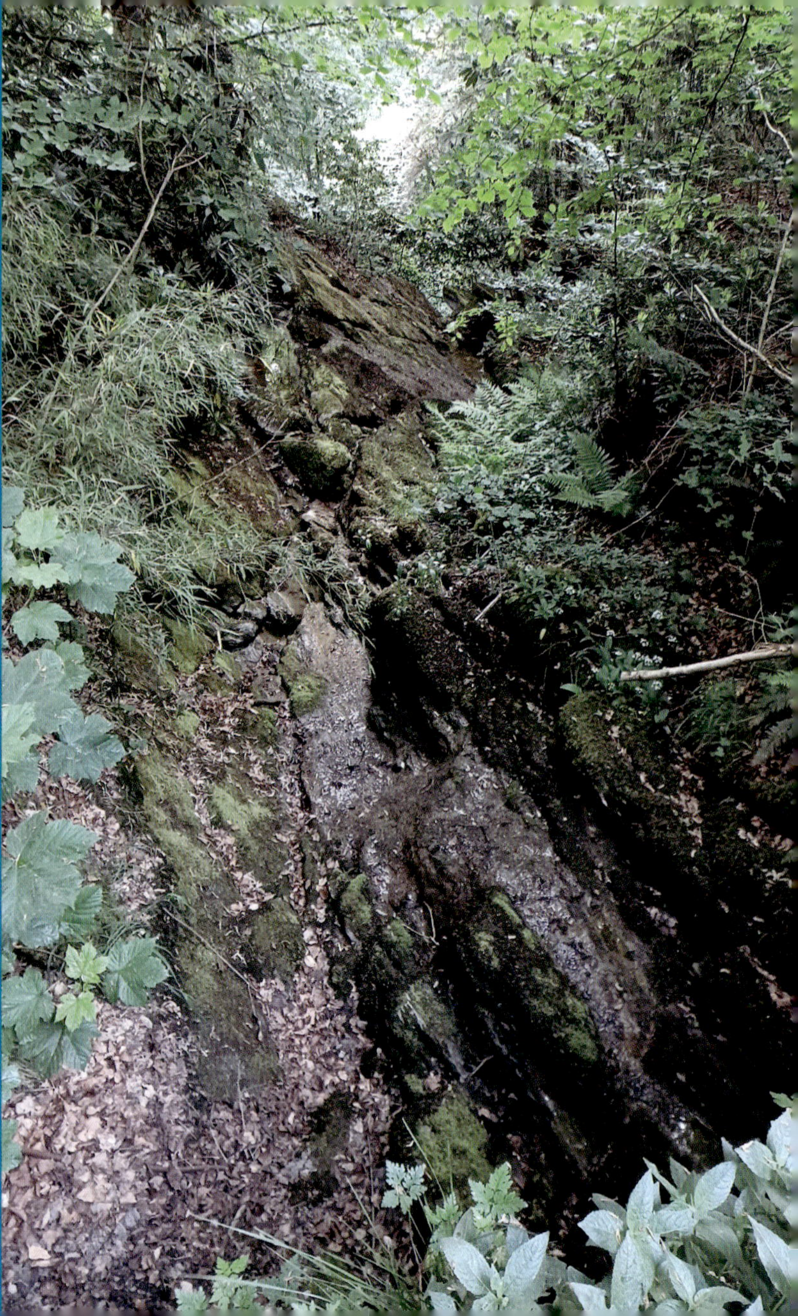

4.8km / 3 miles

01 / INGLEBOROUGH ESTATE NATURE TRAIL FROM CLAPHAM

An accessible, although paid-for, short trip through the Farrers' estate up to Ingleborough show cave.

/ ESSENTIAL INFO
GRADE ●○○○
DISTANCE **4.8KM/3 MILES**
ASCENT **100M**
TIME **1–2 HRS (WALKER)/30–60 MINS (RUNNER)**
START/FINISH **CLAPHAM**
START GRID REF **SD 745 691**
START GPS **54.1171, -2.3915**
OS MAP **OL2 YORKSHIRE DALES: SOUTHERN & WESTERN AREAS (1:25,000)**

/ OVERVIEW
While the Dales are lovely, it's difficult to find accessible tracks. Not only is this nature trail accessible, but there's also a powered mobility scooter available from The Old Sawmill cafe for those without their own. The show cave, owned and run by the same people as the cafe, is one of the very few suitable for wheelchair access. However, be aware there is a charge for using the trail and extra for accessing the cave. See ***www.ingleboroughcave.co.uk*** for current prices and details.

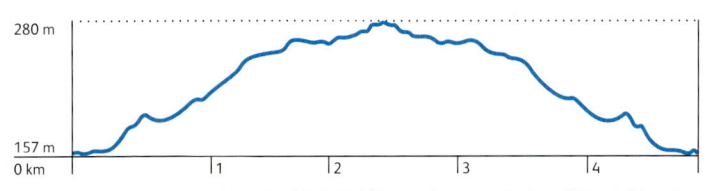

Previous page: Crina Bottom and Ingleborough. Left: Cat Hole Sike unconformity near Clapham. © Hannah Collingridge

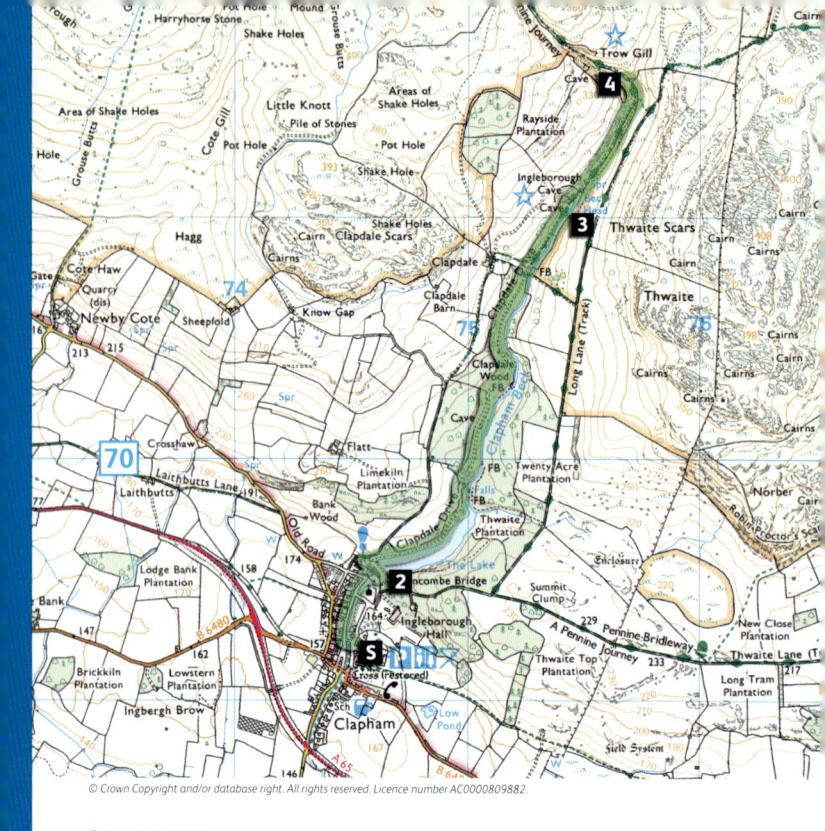

/ DIRECTIONS

S Head **north** alongside the river through Clapham, following signposts for *Ingleborough Cave*. Continue on to The Old Sawmill cafe to pay your entrance fee for the cave.

2 **Enter the trail** and keep going until you reach the show cave, exploring as you go. Along the way, the information boards explain some of the features of the estate. Also, for a bit of full-on Victoriana, there's a folly known as Aunt Bessie's Grotto.

3 Take some time to look around Ingleborough Cave. Afterwards, continue **straight ahead** on the same track – which now becomes rougher – up the dale and round the corner to the bottom of Trow Gill, a great example of a limestone gorge cut towards the end of the last ice age by meltwater.

4 After exploring Trow Gill, **retrace your steps** back to Clapham.

2 | MOUNTAIN WALKS **YORKSHIRE THREE PEAKS**

/GOOD TO KNOW

PUBLIC TRANSPORT AND ACCESS

Clapham railway station is 2.5km from Clapham. Craven Connection bus 581 connects Clapham along the A65 between Kirkby Lonsdale and Settle.

There is a national park pay and display car park with toilets in Clapham, plus some extra parking around the village. All parking gets very busy at weekends and during the summer. There are also some disabled parking spots at The Old Sawmill cafe at the start of the trail.

WHEN TO WALK IT

The track through the nature trail is well maintained and surfaced so it's suitable all year round.

TERRAIN AND NAVIGATION

Well-maintained gravel track with gentle gradients except for one short steeper section near the cafe. It's pretty much uphill all the way and then downhill all the way back. Navigation is very straightforward.

FACILITIES AND REFRESHMENTS

Toilets available in the car park in Clapham. There's a cracking little village shop selling many things to eat, along with cafes and pubs in the village. The Old Sawmill cafe at the trailhead has toilets for customers.

DOGS AND KIDS

Dogs are welcome on a lead. Eminently suitable for small kids as it's also easy enough to take a pushchair along the path.

POINTS OF INTEREST

Information boards along the nature trail point out things along the way such as an artificial lake which was dammed around 1830; this not only provided a fashionable landscape feature but also ensured a constant water supply for the village. The rhododendrons were brought to the estate in the early 20th century by botanist Reginald Farrer; they grow on an outcrop of slate underlying the limestone which can also be glimpsed in Cat Hole Sike. This is also an example of a geological unconformity – there's a missing gap of about 100 million years in the rock deposition.

Ingleborough Cave was first explored – by candlelight – in 1837. More exploration started to show the extent of the system

Aunt Bessie's Grotto. © Hannah Collingridge

under the fell. Dye testing showed that water from Gaping Gill emerged here, and in 1983 cavers made their way between the two caves for the first time. There's even a film by Sid Perou of the breakthrough which is available online.

From the bridge just past the show cave you can see where the underground stream emerges from the fellside. The stream round the cave is also suitable for paddling and playing in.

ALTERNATIVE ACCESSIBLE ROUTE

It's possible to access Hull Pot from Horton in Ribblesdale if you have a suitable off-road mobility scooter, although the track up is much rougher than the maintained nature trail at Clapham.

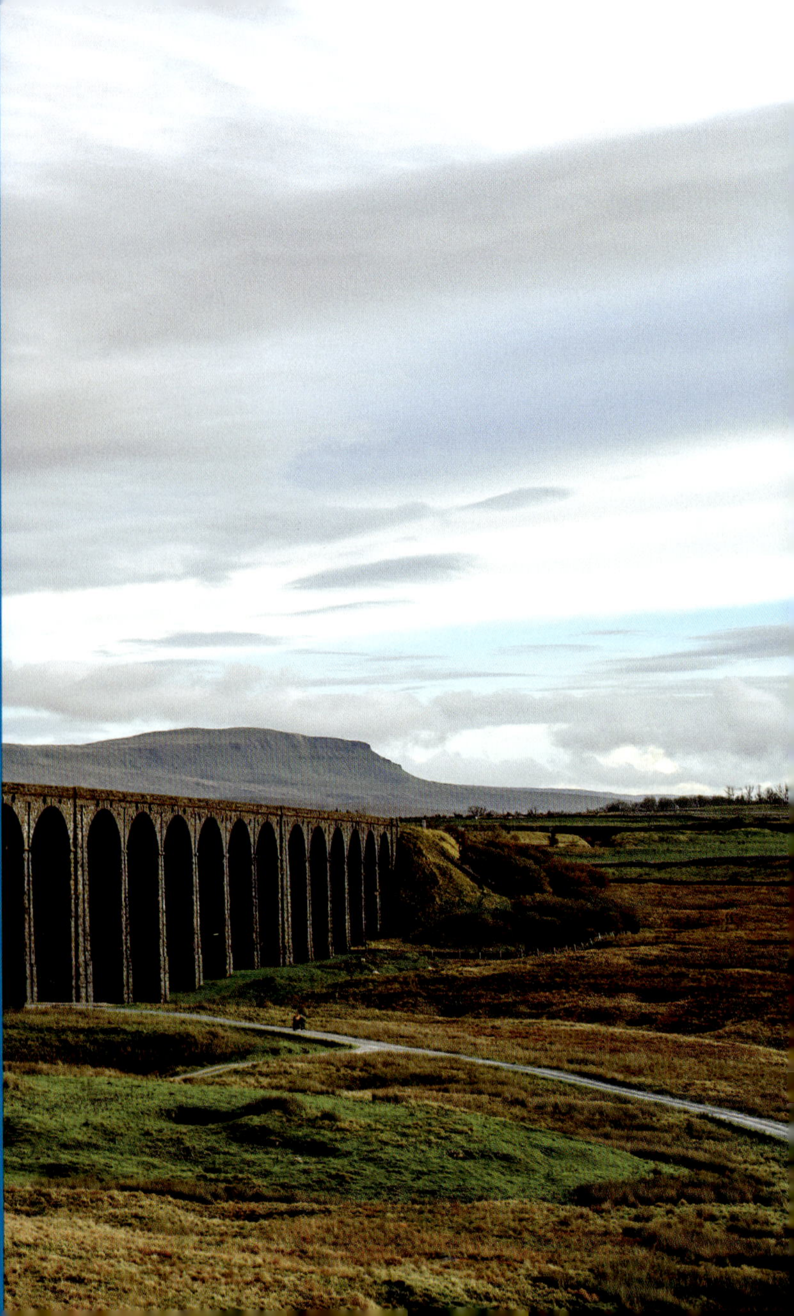

6.2km / 3.9 miles

02 / AROUND RIBBLEHEAD

A short, fascinating jaunt around Ribblehead and the railway.

/ ESSENTIAL INFO
GRADE ●○○○○
DISTANCE **6.2KM/3.9 MILES**
ASCENT **80M**
TIME **1.5–3 HRS (WALKER)/30–60 MINS (RUNNER)**
START/FINISH **RIBBLEHEAD STATION**
START GRID REF **SD 765 789**
START GPS **54.2057, -2.3609**
OS MAP **OL2 YORKSHIRE DALES: SOUTHERN & WESTERN AREAS (1:25,000)**

/ OVERVIEW
A very straightforward walk in terms of terrain and navigation with not a great deal of ascent, but a fascinating look at the famous Ribblehead (Batty Moss) viaduct and some of the remains from the construction of the railway. Even if you choose not to arrive by train, it's worth having a look at Ribblehead station, voted number 2 in the *Sunday Times*' list of 'The UK's loveliest railway stations'. There's a cafe and exhibition during the summer season.

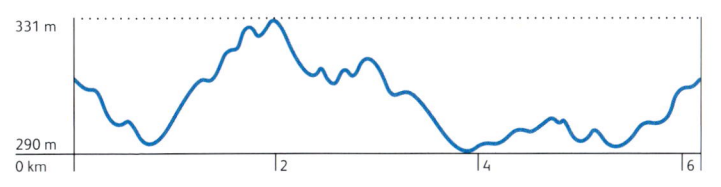

Ribblehead (Batty Moss) viaduct and Pen-y-ghent.

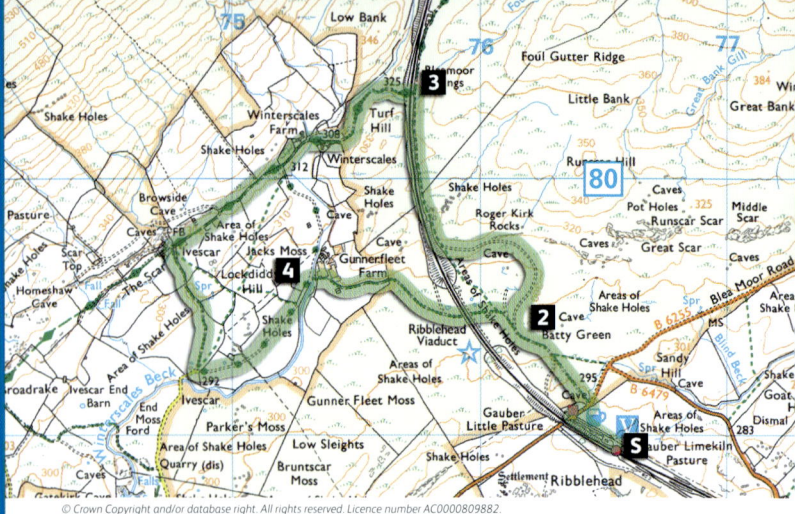

© Crown Copyright and/or database right. All rights reserved. Licence number AC0000809882.

/ DIRECTIONS

S Leave the platform through the signed gate. On your left are the battered remains of a loco chimney as a memorial to the Hawes Junction crash in 1910 and a bit of information about the crash and why the chimney is here. **Keep left** down the entrance road and turn **right** when you meet the main road opposite the pub. Turn **left** on to the large gravelled track just as the wall finishes. The lumps and bumps on the grassy section heading down to the Horton road are part of one of the navvy settlements from the railway construction. Head along the gravel track until you come to a broad grassy track on your right.

2 Turn **right** up this delightful track which is the line of one of the tramways built while construction of the railway was in progress. Below you on the left are the remains of housing, a quarry, loco works, a lime kiln and other buildings. The tramway forks – either path will take you to the main Whernside path, although the right-hand path is likely to be wetter. Once back at the main path, turn **right** and continue to the second of the two arches under the railway line – this track is clearly signposted as a bridleway to Winterscales. You'll get a glimpse of the signal box, still in use, ahead on the main line.

3 Turn **left** and follow the track, rough in places, down to the farm and continue **straight ahead** on the now tarmacked track. At Ivescar farm there is a great junction of paths – turn **left** and keep to the main track. At the next junction turn **left** through the gate, signposted, and head towards the viaduct. Behind you are Whernside and the whole Ingleborough massif – Pen-y-ghent can't be spotted from here; that's Cam End to the side of the viaduct.

6 | MOUNTAIN WALKS **YORKSHIRE THREE PEAKS**

GOOD TO KNOW

PUBLIC TRANSPORT AND ACCESS
Ribblehead is on the Settle–Carlisle railway, with trains to Leeds and Carlisle. There's parking at Ribblehead around the road junction. All parking gets very busy at weekends and during the summer. Please don't drive up to the viaduct as it's a protected site.

WHEN TO WALK IT
Best saved for a day with visibility as the views are far ranging but can be done as a quick leg stretch to justify sloping off for cake and coffee on a very wet day.

TERRAIN AND NAVIGATION
Clear, waymarked tracks, mostly firm underfoot, plus a lovely green old tramway.

FACILITIES AND REFRESHMENTS
The Station Inn at Ribblehead provides Portaloos in the car park, plus a water tap, for the use of walkers. They are (at the time of writing) open for food from 12–9 p.m. If you use their facilities, please contribute to their running costs. There's a seasonal tea room at the station.

DOGS AND KIDS
Livestock and ground-nesting birds mean Ribblehead is a dog-on-lead kind of place, particularly between 1 March and 31 July when it is the law under the CRoW Act that dogs must be on short leads. There's nothing inherently hazardous for kids.

POINTS OF INTEREST
It's really hard to imagine Ribblehead before the railway and the viaduct were built. On this walk, there's a stroll up an old tramway which swings round the remains of the railway construction site, plus views of the viaduct from all sides, including underneath, as well as the surrounding hills.

Work started on the viaduct for the Midland Railway in 1870 and it opened to goods traffic in 1875, passengers in 1876. There are 24 arches, each of a 45-foot span, making this the longest structure on the Settle–Carlisle railway. You may notice that every sixth arch is thicker. It's officially known as Batty Moss viaduct after the area it crosses, but universally known now as Ribblehead. Working and living conditions were pretty basic and records show over 100 men died during the construction. Many workers, and their families, are buried at the church in Chapel-le-Dale where there is also a memorial to them. It's also the reason the railway came very close to closure in the 1980s as the cost of repairs to the structure were deemed prohibitive by British Rail, but a huge public campaign spearheaded by the Friends of the Settle-Carlisle Line managed to prevent the closure. Both the viaduct and the remains of the works around it are now scheduled monuments.

4 At the next road junction in front of the farm buildings, turn **right** towards the viaduct and follow this all the way under the viaduct and back to the road. Retrace your steps **right** then **left** to get back to the station.

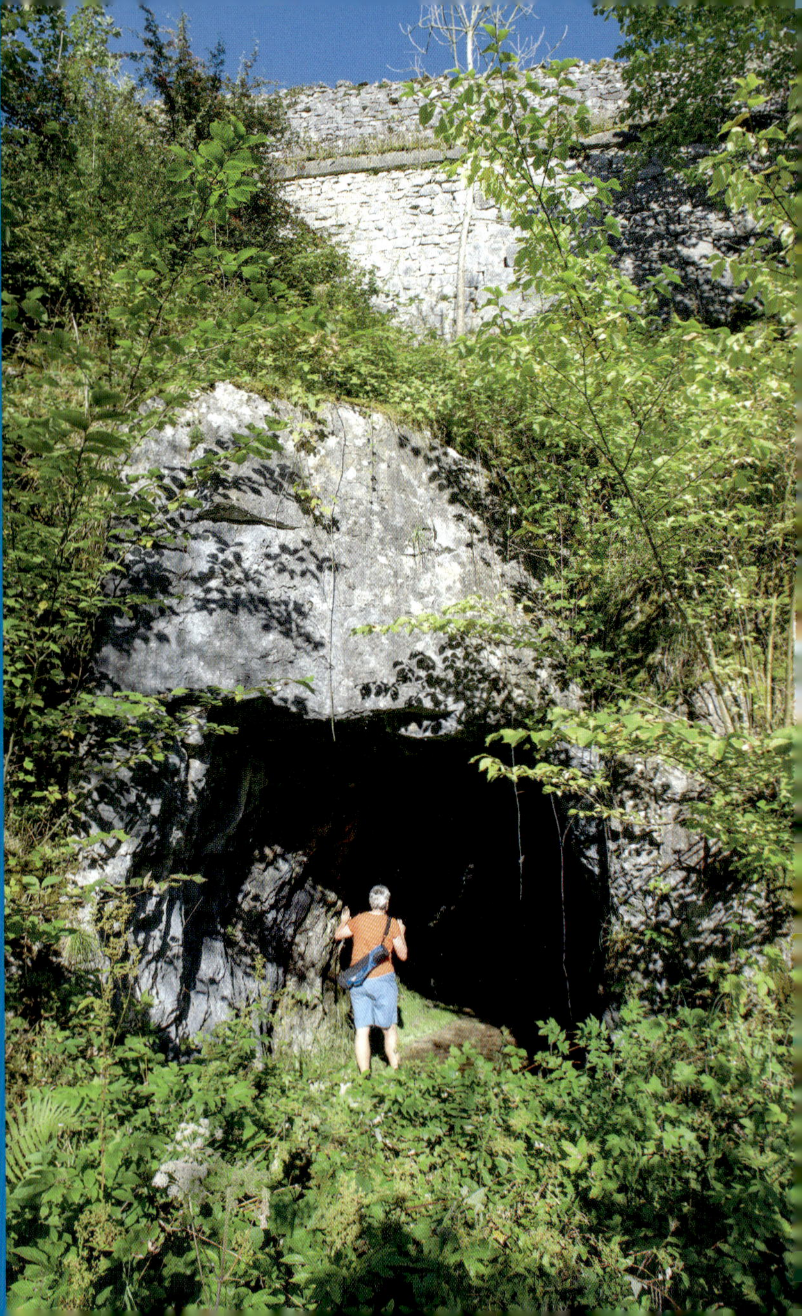

5km / 3.1 miles

03 / STAINFORTH SCAR & THE LIME KILNS

Allow plenty of time for this short but fascinating walk.

/ ESSENTIAL INFO
GRADE ●●○○
DISTANCE **5KM/3.1 MILES**
ASCENT **130M**
TIME **1–3 HRS (WALKER)/30–60 MINS (RUNNER)**
START/FINISH **STAINFORTH YDNP PAY & DISPLAY CAR PARK**
START GRID REF **SD 820 672**
START GPS **54.1003, -2.2767**
OS MAP **OL2 YORKSHIRE DALES: SOUTHERN & WESTERN AREAS (1:25,000)**

/ OVERVIEW
A steepish climb up Stainforth Scar not only gives great views but perspective on how high the scar is. A steep descent brings you back down and round to the fascinating and underrated industrial landscape of the Craven Lime Works – there is an optional trail to see the site. Allow plenty of time for exploration before gently heading back to Stainforth.

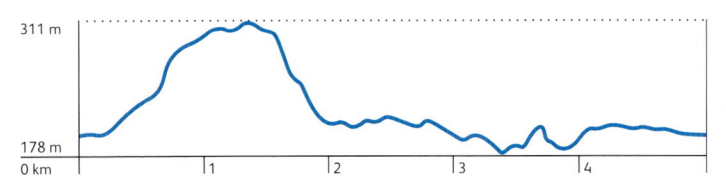

Triple draw kiln.

Stainforth Scar.

/ DIRECTIONS

S **Turn right** out of the car park and follow the main road through the village round over the bridge towards the Craven Heifer. **Turn left** up the small road opposite the pub. Shortly afterwards, **turn right then immediately turn left** to pick up a signposted path (*Winskill 5/8 mile*). At the top of this tiny road, which looks like someone's driveway, **turn right** through a gate and follow the track. There is a short, walled section before it opens out into a short field to reach another gate.

2 Go through the gate and keep following the grassy track which starts out quite broad. There are several tracks through this pasture but **keep to the leftmost path**, heading upwards towards the wood (there should also be a confirmatory post encouraging you towards the left-hand fence line). This path brings you to a gate leading into the wood. Go through the gate and follow the limestone-stepped path which climbs, steeply at times, through the wood. Cross over a ladder stile and out on to the more open land above Stainforth Scar. Continue for a short distance to reach a path junction.

3 **Keep right** at the junction and continue on, crossing a wall into the next field. Keep following the path which brings you to a signpost and a short scramble down or round to a stile. Cross the stile and go **straight ahead** through the Lower Winskill farmyard to pick up a track, **heading right** at a junction to stay on the main track. Continue along the track until it opens out on the left-hand side and look for a footpath on the **right** signed for *Langcliffe*. Head through the stile and gate combo and follow the grassy path through the field. At the far end of the field, you enter an odd, almost triangular, short field – head **right** on the path and keep **straight on** past a cairn for the descent. The path heads

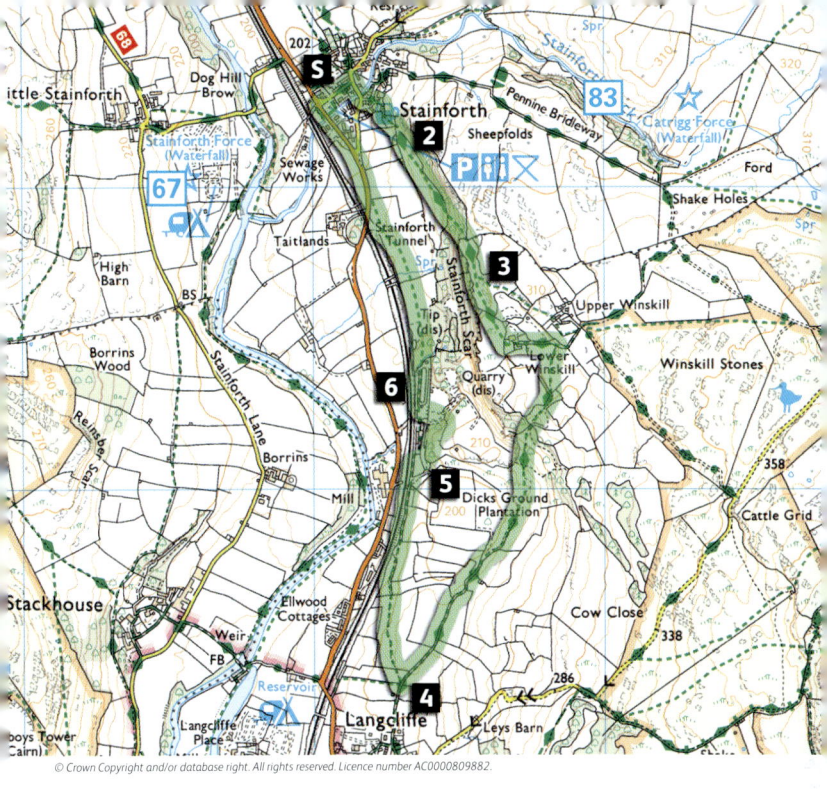

© Crown Copyright and/or database right. All rights reserved. Licence number AC0000809882.

down straight before another wall where it swings round **leftwards** but is clear to follow. A very short section of walled track leads to a delightful grassy terrace – great for a short break and contemplation of the views. The track becomes walled – follow it until you reach a junction at SD 823 653.

4 At the junction **turn sharp right** on to a field path (signposted *Stainforth*), heading almost back the way you came. Follow this clear path through several terraced fields until it becomes evident you are beginning to run parallel to the railway. Again, the track becomes walled and drops down to a very minor road with a railway arch to your left. Go **straight ahead** up the flight of stairs on the opposite side of the road where there is an information board about the Craven Lime Works. There is a short trail around what remains of the lime works which runs in a figure of eight around the site. The trail is well worth following if you even have a passing interest in industrial remains, although it's worth noting the site is also pretty overgrown and has some steep stair sets made of limestone so can be slippery in the wet.

5 As the path heads towards the new industrial estate look for a dilapidated brick building on the right behind the new units – this is the weighbridge*; **bear right** here for a closer look if you want to. To join the trail round the Craven Lime Works, head **right** (facing the weighbridge) along the road parallel to where you've come from, passing an old sign about parking on the way before taking **a set of limestone steps** into the wood.

> *To miss out the weighbridge and the Craven Lime Works continue **straight on** and rejoin the main route at the Hoffmann kiln.

Head up an inclined plane towards a set of ruins on the right – these are all that remains of the last set of kilns on the site, the Spencer kilns. The inclined plane continues up and round, passing a couple of old rails lying by the side of the track. Ahead you get a glimpse of the quarry face through the trees. A set of steep limestone steps, thankfully with a rope handrail, takes you back down to the road. **Turn right** where there is a cracking view of the crag, round into the car park and down the wooden stairs to the Hoffmann kiln.

6 The Hoffmann kiln is the largest one on the site and is well worth exploring. (At the far end of the kiln you can take a short detour and follow the path round to see the remains of the reservoir and tramways – there was even a tramway on top on the kiln for moving raw material to the right spot.) From the end of the kiln take the path leading up and **over the stream**. Follow the path upwards and round to a sign that proclaims *The End of Craven Lime Works*. (From this point you can detour and continue back down the hill to see the triple draw kilns. These are the old-school technology for making lime but you get to see exactly how close the railway was to the site.) To continue to Stainforth **cross into the field** from the sign and follow the path. Pass through a gate and a stream (depending on vegetation you may be able to see the entrance portal to Stainforth Tunnel below on your left). Shortly after the railway disappears the path comes down to the road. **Turn right** and follow the pavement back to Stainforth – the car park is the **second turning on the right**.

The Hoffman kiln.

/ GOOD TO KNOW

PUBLIC TRANSPORT AND ACCESS
DalesBus 11 connects Stainforth with Horton in Ribblesdale and Settle. The national park car park is just off the B6479 between Ribblehead and Settle.

WHEN TO WALK IT
Clear weather gives the stunning views; dry weather makes scrambling round the industrial ruins easier.

TERRAIN AND NAVIGATION
A mixture of surfaces – tarmac, gravel tracks and grassy paths. Steep steps on some parts of the Craven Lime Works trail which can be avoided.

FACILITIES AND REFRESHMENTS
The Craven Heifer pub is in Stainforth village; alternatvely there is a cafe at Knight Stainforth Hall Camping and Caravan Park, near Stainforth Force. There are toilets in the national park car park in Stainforth.

DOGS AND KIDS
Livestock means this is a dog-on-lead kind of walk. Kids (of all ages) will love exploring the lime kilns – as to be expected on an old industrial site there are some hazards, so take appropriate care.

POINTS OF INTEREST
Stainforth Scar may look natural but is actually the remains of a huge quarry. Part of the quarry floor was used as a landfill site between 1967 and 1990, so is much higher than it originally was. Below it sits the Craven Lime Works; the site has the remains of several lime kilns including the huge Hoffmann kiln which you can now walk round. The Hoffmann kiln is rather well preserved and gives an idea of the sheer scale of lime burning that was carried out on site. The building of the famous Settle–Carlisle railway, which the walk follows for a while, made this site economically viable. A reminder that the Dales isn't just about pretty landscapes but has a long history of industry too.

03 / STAINFORTH SCAR & THE LIME KILNS

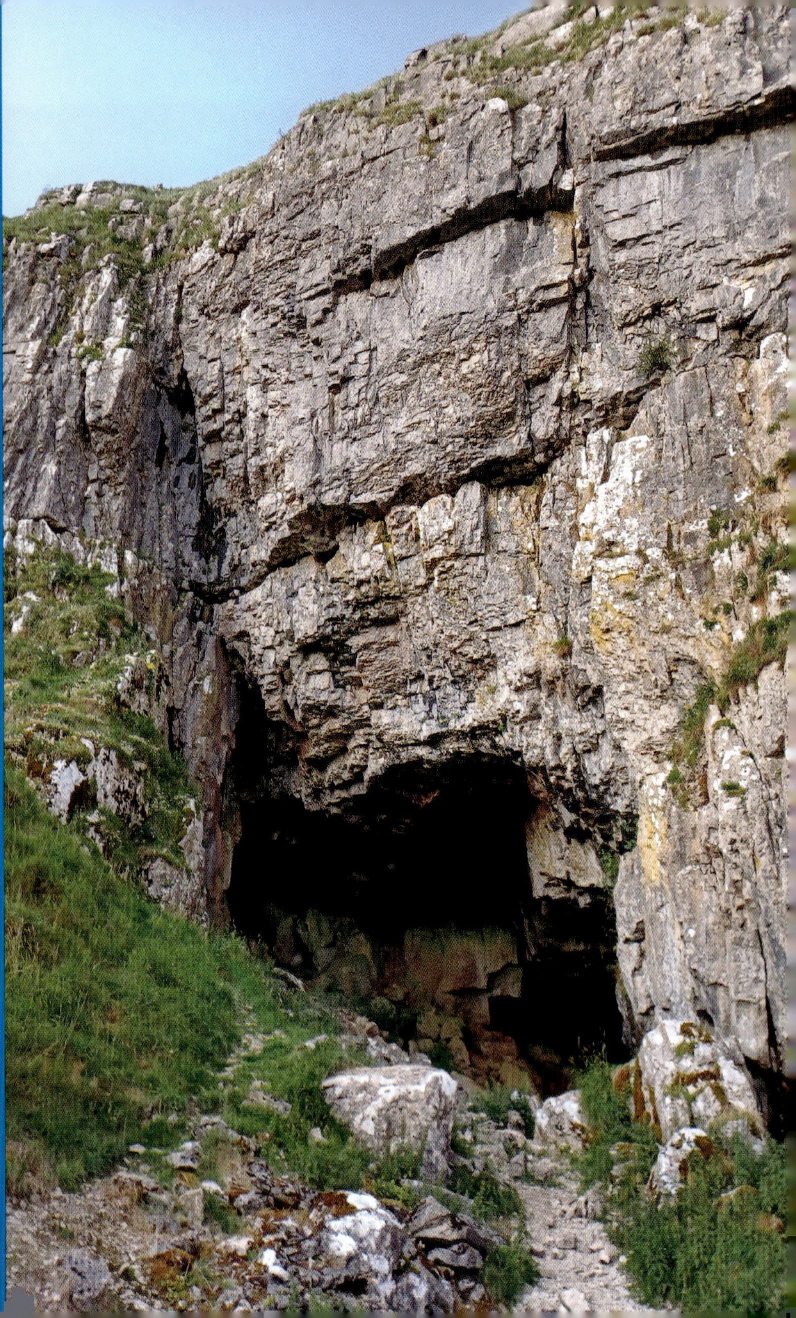

7.1km / 4.4 miles

04 / SETTLE TO ATTERMIRE SCAR & VICTORIA CAVE

A lower-level but scenically stunning walk from the market town of Settle, exploring caves for the non-caver and limestone scenery.

/ ESSENTIAL INFO
GRADE ●●○○
DISTANCE **7.1KM/4.4 MILES**
ASCENT **180M**
TIME **1.5–3 HRS (WALKER)/1 HR (RUNNER)**
START/FINISH **MARKET PLACE, SETTLE**
START GRID REF **SD 819 637**
START GPS **54.0689, -2.2767**
OS MAP **OL2 YORKSHIRE DALES: SOUTHERN & WESTERN AREAS (1:25,000)**

/ OVERVIEW
A steepish pull out of Settle brings you out into the area of amazing limestone scenery around Attermire Scar. Don't be in a rush as there's plenty to explore with several caves suitable for those who have no intention of ever going caving. Take a torch and you'll get glimpses of a whole other world.

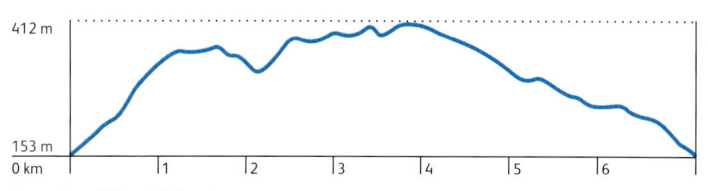

Victoria Cave. © Hannah Collingridge

The back of Warrendale Knotts from Jubilee Cave.

/DIRECTIONS

S Leave the Market Place passing the Co-op, heading **east** on to Constitution Hill, following the road as it narrows and wiggles past houses. Just past a wooden gate on the right, **bear right** on to a walled gravel track (the Pennine Bridleway). Continue climbing on the walled track until you pass through a gate with a stone barn on the left and a clump of trees on the right. **Take the grassy track to the right**, ascending to a broken wall line. Cross the wall line and continue round to the right, heading to another wall at SD 829 640.

2 It's here the options start – there are two delightful grassy paths across the next field. **Take either path and continue straight ahead** to admire Warrendale Knotts from below. (If you want to explore the Knotts, keep to the **left-hand path** then cross a stile on the **left** over a wall before climbing steeply. To descend you can follow sheep trods across the top of the cliff.) All paths meet up again at or before a junction underneath Attermire Scar at SD 839 641. (Attermire Cave is straight ahead above you. If you want to detour and have a look, take the thin, loose path up the scar and make your way up the grassy and limestone ledges to the entrance.)

© Crown Copyright and/or database right. All rights reserved. Licence number AC0000809882.

Attermire Scar. © Hannah Collingridge

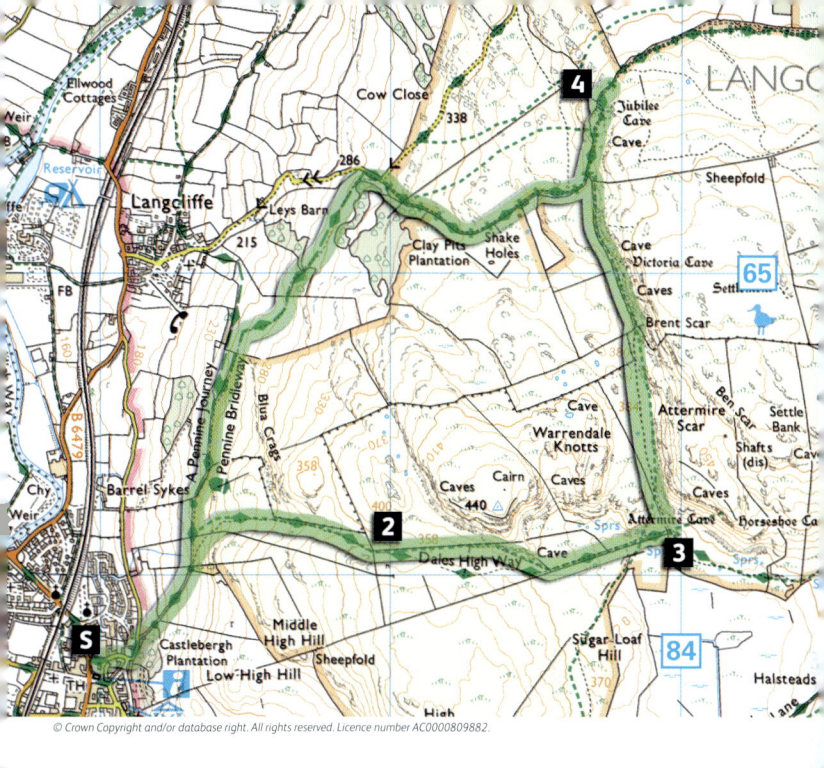

04/ SETTLE TO ATTERMIRE SCAR & VICTORIA CAVE   17

Pen-y-ghent from Jubilee Cave.

3 Turn **left** and follow the obvious path under the scars. (It's worth taking a detour to Victoria Cave – a small path leads off **right** to the obvious entrance. On the small path back to the main path there's another small cave that is accessible if usually a bit moist.) Continue to a gate and track. **Turn right** along the track to reach some more small caves and, if you go up the rise and round the corner to Jubilee Cave, a fantastic view of Pen-y-ghent.

4 After exploring the caves and enjoying the views, **retrace your steps** along the track, carrying on **straight ahead** along the track to reach a road. **Turn left** along the road then **immediately turn left** through a gate, staying on the Pennine Bridleway. Follow the Pennine Bridleway back into Settle, **turning left** on to Constitution Hill to return to Market Place.

GOOD TO KNOW

PUBLIC TRANSPORT AND ACCESS

You can get direct trains to Settle from Leeds. From the west you need to change at Long Preston and travel north to Settle. The Craven Connection (DalesBus) bus services link Settle with nearby towns along the A65.

Settle is bypassed by the A65 – you'll follow the old road into town. There are several pay and display car parks, but the town does get very busy. There is disc parking in the Market Place and surrounding streets (you can't park in the Market Place on Tuesdays when the market is there).

WHEN TO WALK IT

The paths stay mostly dry all year round. This is an absolutely cracking walk late on a summer evening when the golden light hits the scars.

TERRAIN AND NAVIGATION

A mix of limestone and grassy tracks. If you go up to Warrendale Knotts it's a steeper, loose path; the descent on sheep trods is easier.

FACILITIES AND REFRESHMENTS

There are toilets in Whitefriars car park near the start of the walk and plenty of cafes, shops and takeaways in the town.

DOGS AND KIDS

Livestock and ground-nesting birds mean it is a dog-on-lead kind of place, particularly between 1 March and 31 July when it is the law under the CRoW Act that dogs must be on short leads.

This walk is a great choice for fit and adventurous kids, especially as you can safely go a short distance into several caves.

POINTS OF INTEREST

Warrendale Knotts is a stunning series of limestone knolls, full of interest, which can be explored.

Attermire Scar lies right on the line of the Mid Craven Fault and contains several caves including Attermire Cave and Victoria Cave.

Attermire Cave is easy enough to walk into and there's quite a lot that daylight reaches. A little further back it's possible to follow it for a short way if you have a torch. The passage then becomes a squeeze and it's time to turn round or advance only with someone experienced. There are actually 183 metres of passage here. You may notice the keyhole shape of the cave – the higher round bit was formed when the area was below the water table. Later, when the water table dropped, water flowing through the cave cut the lower passage. Now, of course, it's all way above the water table. Finds in Attermire Cave include the remains of a chariot burial.

Victoria Cave was discovered in 1837 by a chap trying to find his dog but who found bones, coins and metal as well. It turned out to be one of the most amazing and important archaeological discoveries in the area with finds dating back 120,000 years, as well as Romano–British artefacts. Weird to think this area was once tropical seas somewhere near the equator. Due to ecological concerns it's not possible to go very far in now but it's worth seeing.

Settle. © Hannah Collingridge

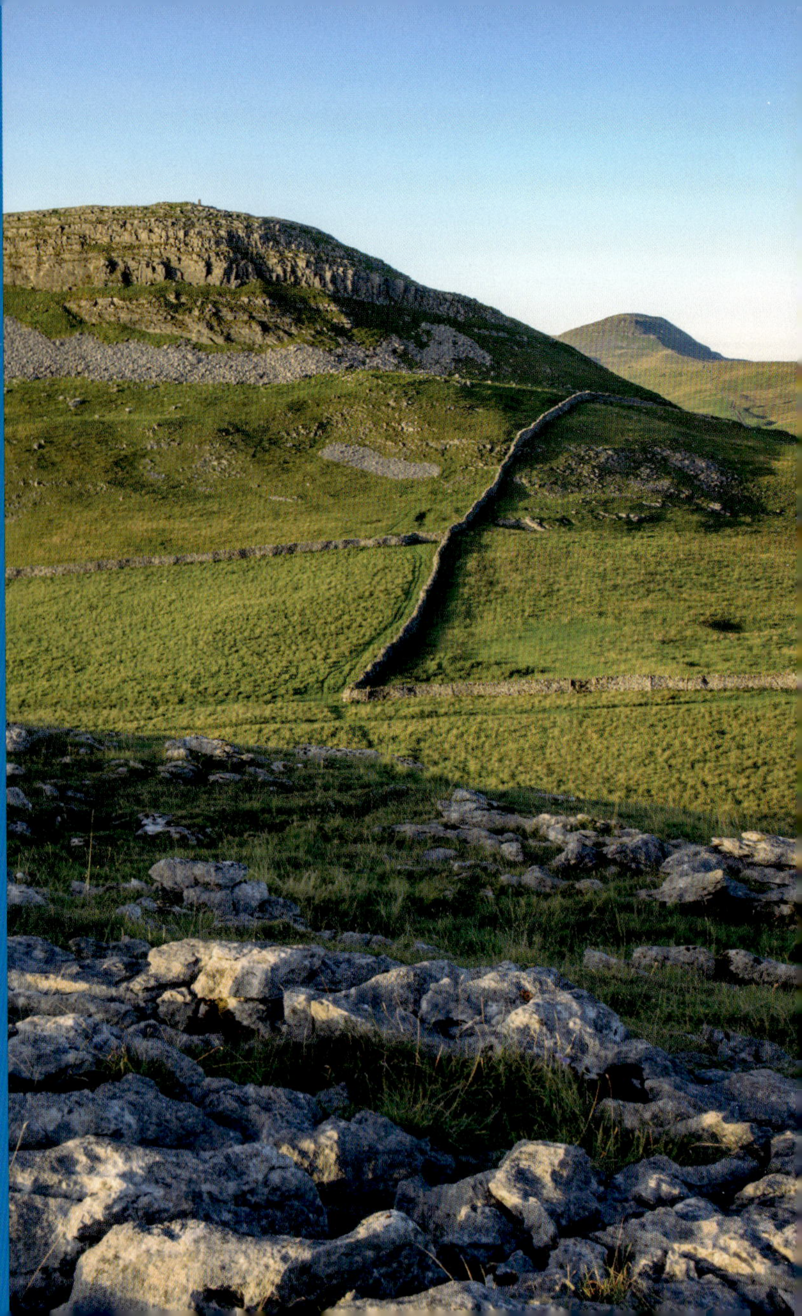

10.2km / 6.3 miles

05 / STAINFORTH & FEIZOR

A cracking lower-level walk through great limestone scenery.

/ ESSENTIAL INFO
GRADE ● ● ○ ○
DISTANCE **10.2KM/6.3 MILES**
ASCENT **250M**
TIME **2–4 HRS (WALKER)/1.25–2.25 HRS (RUNNER)**
START/FINISH **STAINFORTH YDNP PAY & DISPLAY CAR PARK**
START GRID REF **SD 820 672**
START GPS **54.1003, -2.2767**
OS MAP **OL2 YORKSHIRE DALES: SOUTHERN & WESTERN AREAS; OL41 FOREST OF BOWLAND & RIBBLESDALE (BOTH 1:25,000)**

/ OVERVIEW
A steady climb from the River Ribble brings you to Happy Valley then a short ascent takes in the Celtic Wall before crossing the valley to wander over Smearsett and Pot scars. The halfway point at Feizor includes a classic tea room before a choice of return journeys, both of which include the spectacular Stainforth Force.

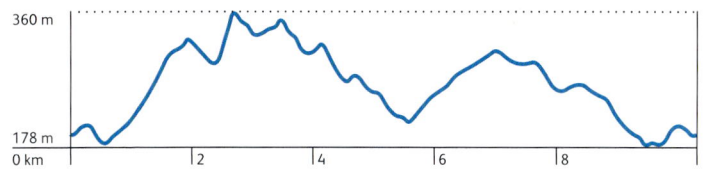

Smearsett Scar and Pen-y-ghent.

Feizor Nick. © Hannah Collingridge

/ DIRECTIONS

S From the car park in Stainforth follow the *Pennine Bridleway* signs to the **bottom left-hand corner of the car park** (with the toilets behind you) to pick up the subway under the main road. Follow the path round and **turn left** at a track. Pass over the railway and keep **straight ahead** into what looks like a dead end; shortly afterwards **turn right** on to a path running parallel to the railway (it's usually very clearly signposted) to reach a road. **Turn left** and head steeply down the narrow road which then crosses the river via an old packhorse bridge (at this point the *No Caravans* signs make perfect sense). Head up the hill on the road, past the campsite on the left and a hall on the right to reach a crossroads. (The hall you have just passed is a former manor house; it's an older site but this house dates to 1672 with later tweaks and adjustments. There's been a campsite here since the 1920s.)

2 Go **straight ahead** at the crossroads following the Dales High Way (the Pennine Bridleway turns off right here) and carry on through a gate and along a short section of walled track to reach a junction of tracks – go **straight ahead** on to a track, still heading uphill. The stony track ends but there is a wide grassy track to follow through the limestone on either side. Continue over a stile, climb a bit more and then the track begins to dip down. Ahead is Happy Valley. You should have stunning views of Pen-y-ghent to your right and your more immediate destinations of Smearsett Scar and Pot Scar ahead and to the right. Up on the left-hand side is the Celtic Wall.

05/STAINFORTH & FEIZOR   23

Stainforth packhorse bridge.

3 Keep going **straight ahead** along the broad grassy track then cross a stile over a wall; the path continues parallel to the wall. (If you want to visit the Celtic Wall then **turn left** and follow a trod across the marshier ground to a gate and then pick your way up the scar. Return to the same point in the valley.) Follow the path to the next cross wall (on the right) and turn **right**, following the wall and leaving the Dales High Way. Continue **straight ahead** to reach a wall corner and stile at SD 802 676. Cross the stile and go **straight ahead**, following the wall as the path rises. At the top of the slope look for a path on the **left** heading upwards – there are plenty of sheep trods and as long as you head upwards you will arrive at the trig point on Smearsett Scar.

4 From the trig point continue **straight ahead** and follow the thin paths on top of Smearsett and Pot scars, exploring the stunning scenery. There is a drop in between Smearsett and Pot scars – follow whichever path you find comfortable and aim for the stone step-through stile (not always easy to spot). It is fairly close to the cliff edge near where there is a bit of fence on top of the wall. Continue along the top of Pot Scar and its cairns before heading onwards. The path drops into a hollow with longer grass – do not be tempted by the cairn on the scar ahead as there is a large wall in the way. Follow the path round to the **right** to reach a stile.

24 | MOUNTAIN WALKS **YORKSHIRE THREE PEAKS**

Stainforth Force.

5 Cross the stile and take some time to wander to your heart's content exploring the limestone. Whichever way you go – it's simplest to head **straight ahead** from the stile – you need to end up at the bottom of the field where there is a stile at Feizor Nick (SD 790 684). **Turn left** and follow the Pennine Bridleway into Feizor.

6 Walk through the village to reach Elaine's Tea Rooms* and continue **straight ahead**.

> *For a shorter route back, from the tea rooms **turn left** on to the Dales High Way through Happy Valley (signposted *Stainforth*), admiring the skyline you came along. Rejoin and retrace the outward route from 3.

Cross the (usually dry) ford and **turn left** on to a bridleway (signposted *Scar Top*). There are actually several tracks across the pastureland but keep roughly in the middle and they all meet up again. At a signpost where the bridleway goes to the right, go **straight ahead** on to a footpath. This stretch gives you chance to admire the cunning use of materials recycled into gates and stiles by local farmers. There is a striking example that I originally took to be an old bedstead but isn't. Continue on and go through a gateway to reach a path junction at (SD 804 664).

05/STAINFORTH & FEIZOR

View down Happy Valley towards Feizor.

7 At the junction, one path goes off through the right-hand wall and on towards Stackhouse and there are two going **straight ahead** and remaining on this side of the wall – follow either of these two paths (they join back up at the bottom corner of the field). Continue **straight ahead** as you are funnelled along a short walled track into a sheep holding area. Admire the farmer's creative use of ironmongery and head over **a stile on the left-hand wall**. With the wall behind you go **straight ahead** across the field, past a fingerpost and on to a gate where the track become more clearly defined. This track meets the outward route at a junction.

8 **Turn right** at the junction along a walled track which becomes a road to reach the crossroads in Little Stainforth. Go **straight ahead** then just before the packhorse bridge use the stile or gate on the **right** to follow the river a short distance to Stainforth Force. There are three short falls and then a deep plunge pool – well known as a swimming location. If lucky you may see traditional mating rituals in action – the boys leap off higher and higher parts of the bank and the girls in the pool below ignore them.

9 Retrace your steps back to the road, **turn right** to cross the bridge and head up the steep road of Dog Hill Brow. **Turn right** on to the Pennine Bridleway just before the main road. Follow the signs and your outward journey back to the car park.

/ GOOD TO KNOW

PUBLIC TRANSPORT AND ACCESS

DalesBus 11 connects Stainforth with Horton in Ribblesdale and Settle. The national park car park is just off the B6479 between Ribblehead and Settle.

WHEN TO WALK IT

This walk is best with good visibility because the views are stunning. There are a few places on the walk that will get muddy after a wet spell but mostly it's pretty well drained.

TERRAIN AND NAVIGATION

A mix of clear and obvious footpaths with narrow grassy trods – which may disappear – on top of the scars. The tops of Smearsett and Pot scars aren't easy to navigate in mist.

FACILITIES AND REFRESHMENTS

The Craven Heifer pub is in Stainforth village; alternatvely there is a cafe at Knight Stainforth Hall Camping and Caravan Park, near Stainforth Force. Elaine's Tea Rooms are in Feizor and a welcome stop halfway round. There are toilets in the national park car park in Stainforth.

Limestone pavement on Pot Scar, Ingleborough in the distance.

DOGS AND KIDS

Livestock and ground-nesting birds mean it is a dog-on-lead kind of place, particularly between 1 March and 31 July when it is the law under the CRoW Act that dogs must be on short leads.

This walk is a good option for kids, as there is nothing particularly hazardous and it can be cut shorter from Feizor if necessary.

POINTS OF INTEREST

The Celtic Wall is interesting to see, if mysterious. The name may be misleading, as the dating of such a feature is nigh on impossible. There's a longer section of wall, and a shorter and smaller bit to the side – it's a bit of a mystery as it doesn't seem to have any function. However, it's a good viewpoint.

Smearsett and Pot scars are some of the distinctive lumps you see so often in the Dales but can never quite name. It's great to visit them and put a name to a face.

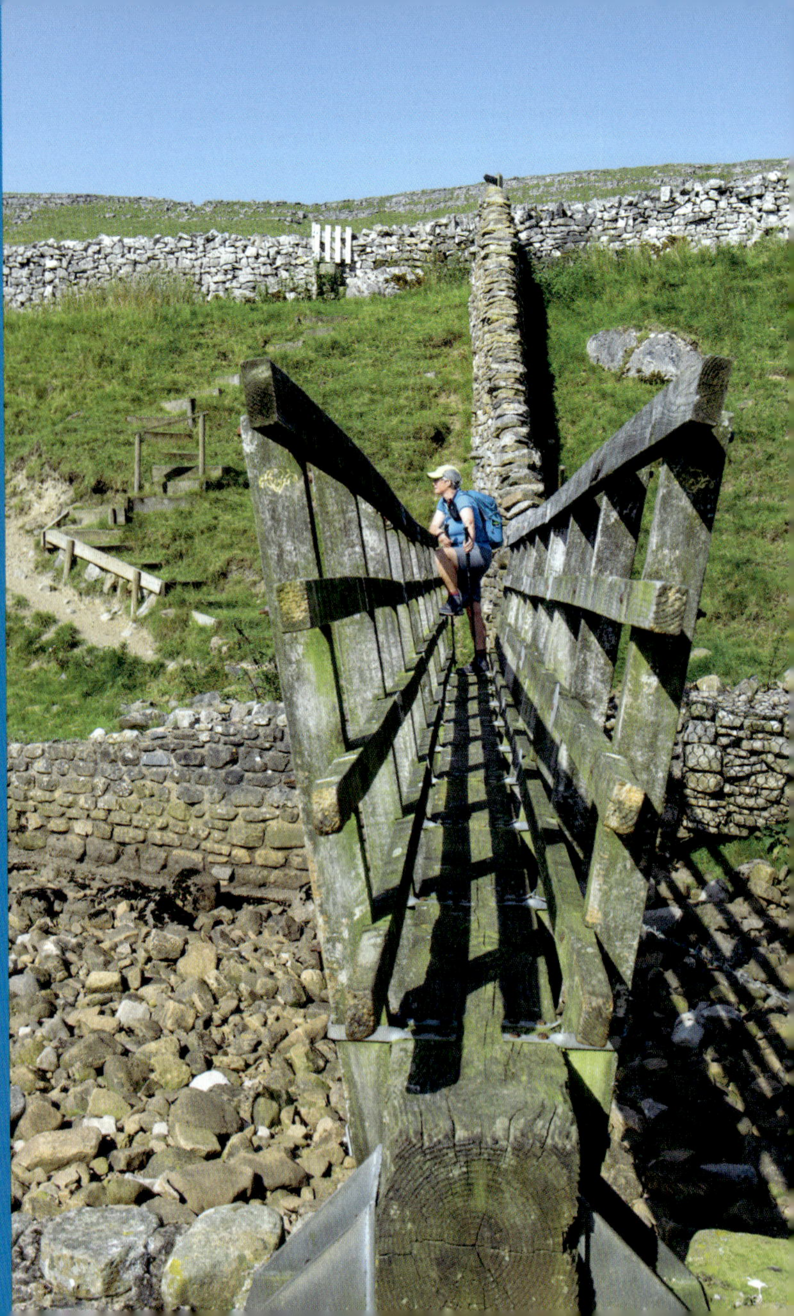

11.5km / 7.1 miles

06 / YORDAS CAVE & TURBARY ROAD

A lower-level walk and the chance to visit caves suitable for non-cavers.

/ ESSENTIAL INFO
GRADE ●●○○
DISTANCE **11.5KM/7.1 MILES**
ASCENT **260M**
TIME **2.5–5 HRS (WALKER)/1.25–2.25 HRS (RUNNER)**
START/FINISH **LAY-BY ON THORNTON LANE, 2KM NORTH OF THORNTON IN LONSDALE**
START GRID REF **SD 691 756**
START GPS **54.1752, -2.4748**
OS MAP **OL2 YORKSHIRE DALES: SOUTHERN & WESTERN AREAS (1:25,000)**

/ OVERVIEW
A quieter walk exploring the glacial valley of Kingsdale with a visit to an old Victorian show cave – bring the best torch you possess – and the return journey along an old peat road right along the line of many potholes and caves.

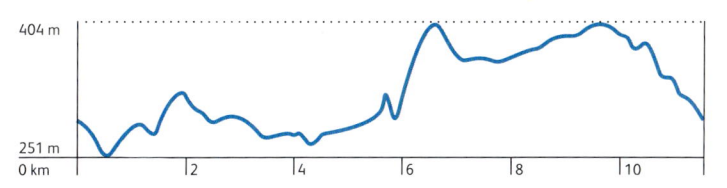

Footbridge in Kingsdale.

The lovely glacial dumping at Raven Ray diverting the river.

/ DIRECTIONS

S From the lay-by head north along the road (away from Thornton in Lonsdale) then after 400m **turn right** along a walled track. Stay on the track as it passes through a gate, over the stream, and climbs. The track levels off and becomes open fell on the left-hand side. **Turn left** along another track going back on yourself heading upwards and follow the wall. (The path you have just come past with *No Entry* signs on it comes in from the famous Ingleton Waterfalls Trail. This starts in Ingleton and has an admission charge but is of great interest and includes Thornton Force.)

2 Go **straight ahead** over a stile, across a short field to another wall and stile, and follow the path along the side of Wackenburgh Hill. Crossing another wall leads into rough pasture which can get soggy after wet weather – follow the wall line to a gate. Then it's **straight ahead** through three less rough fields – the only challenge is trying to spot the stile in the wall on the other side. In the third field head for the **left-hand side of the house**. A small enclosure is exited on the right, then **turn left** through the yard, **right** on the track and then **left** up the banking to a stile. (Following the track through a gate brings you to the same place but it isn't the right of way.) In practice this section is less complicated than it sounds as it's usually all signposted.

06 / YORDAS CAVE & TURBARY ROAD 31

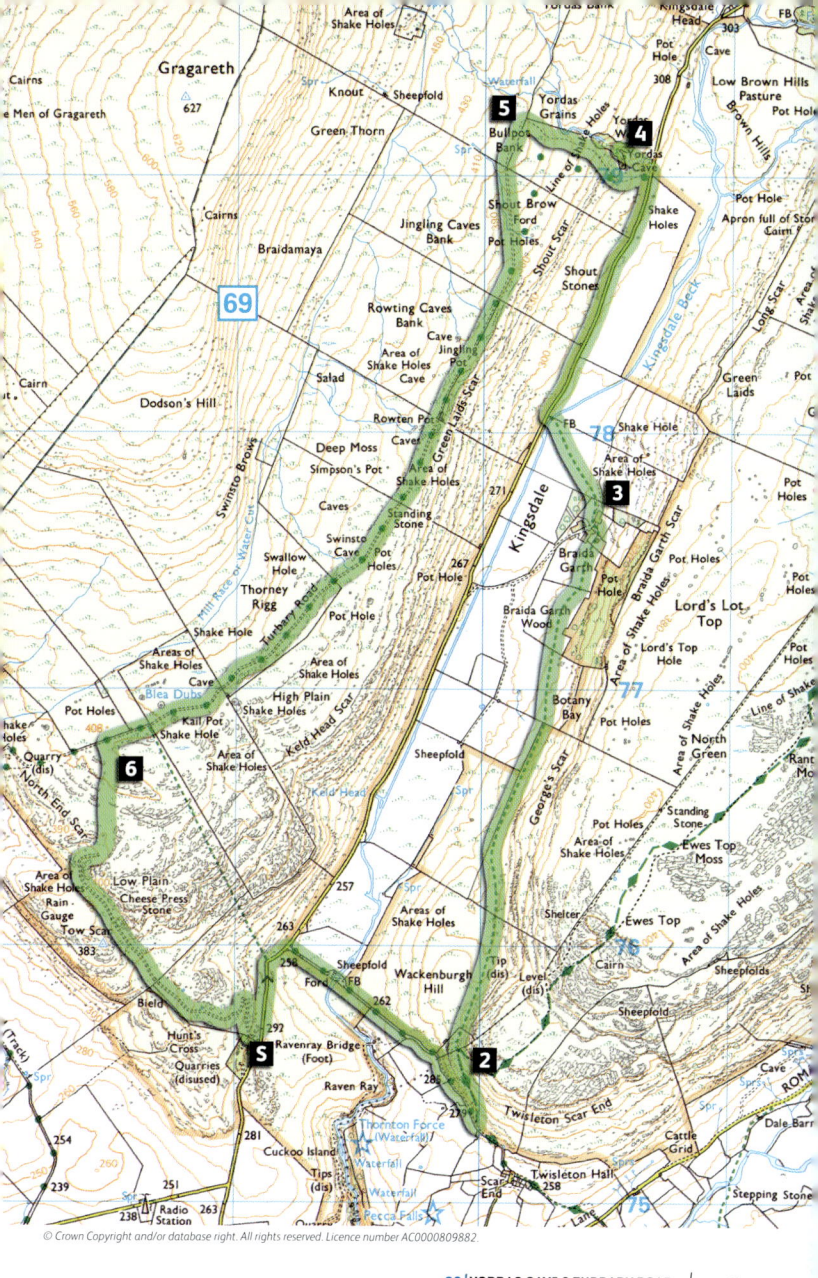

3 Head **diagonally across the field** to a footbridge in the **north-west** corner and go up some steps to reach a lane. **Turn right** along the lane. Follow the lane for about 1km and **turn left** through a gate with *Access Only* signs on it opposite a lay-by. Head up the path on the **right-hand side of the dry riverbed** and go through a gate to the entrance to Yordas Cave, which is well worth exploring.

4 After exploring the cave*, return to the gate by the road and take the path on the **left-hand side of the dry riverbed** to reach a gate at SD 701 792.

> *If you're up for something different, you can **scramble up the dry limestone gill** above the cave. This is a nice straightforward scramble suitable for most, with plenty of escape routes either side. There are several pothole entrances along the way to peer into as well. Where the water appears, head up the **left-hand side of the stream** and follow it to the wall – you can safely get round the wall without causing damage at the streambed. (This is a nice paddling spot on a fine day.) Head up the **left-hand side of the wall** to a gate at SD 701 792, either directly or by heading further left to pick up the path.

5 **Turn left** through the gate – this is Turbary Road and it's straightforward to follow along the limestone shelf. The most obvious cave along the road is Rowten Pot; it sits right on the path just after a gate at SD 698 780. Possibly surprisingly it's unfenced, so peer into its depths with caution. You can also peer into the eyehole next to it too. (If you follow the dry streambed uphill a short way you'll come across the Rowten Caves system which are easy to explore with sense, caution and a good torch. The easiest entrance is the highest one up the hill, and it leads into a delightful sinuous passage it's possible to walk through.)

6 Continue along Turbary Road to SD 684 767 exploring the other caves and potholes along the road as much or as little as you like. Pick up a grassy path heading **left** to start descending to the road. The path becomes more track like and steeper before emerging on to the road and the starting lay-by.

GOOD TO KNOW

PUBLIC TRANSPORT AND ACCESS

There's no public transport to Kingsdale so you'll have to use your car or walk up from Ingleton. Access to Kingsdale is from Thornton in Lonsdale just off the A65. The suggested lay-by is a couple of miles from the A65. It does get busy up here – there's the odd alternative parking spot along Thornton Lane but not many.

WHEN TO WALK IT

The eastern side of the valley does get soggy after a lot of rain and can be cut up by cows. Otherwise, everything drains quite well. There's enough of immediate interest on a low-visibility day to make a good walk but you'd miss out on cracking views.

TERRAIN AND NAVIGATION

Some slightly sketchy paths through farmland, a lot of good tracks and an optional scramble. Navigation is pretty straightforward.

FACILITIES AND REFRESHMENTS

The Marton Arms pub is in Thornton in Lonsdale, otherwise Ingleton has toilets and refreshments of all kinds. In season there is often an ice cream van around Twisleton Scar for the people doing the Ingleton Waterfalls Trail.

DOGS AND KIDS

Livestock and ground-nesting birds mean it is a dog-on-lead kind of place, particularly between 1 March and 31 July when it is the law under the CRoW Act that dogs must be on short leads.

This can be a great choice for fit and adventurous kids especially as you can safely go a short distance into some caves and peer into many potholes. Be aware that some potholes are very deep and unfenced.

POINTS OF INTEREST

Wackenburgh Hill is moraine left by the last glacier which blocked the end of the valley. A lake formed behind it, eventually bursting through the moraine at its weakest point – hence the weird kink in the riverbed.

Yordas Cave used to be a Victorian show cave, hence the shape of the entrance way. Not far inside the entrance is a large cavern with a stream running through it. At the right-hand end of the cavern is the Chapter House which has a splendid waterfall. The cave has a good Scandinavian name, too: *Jörð á*, meaning 'earth stream'.

The word 'turbary' means the ancient right to cut turf or peat for fuel – hence the name of Turbary Road, which was used by the people of Thornton in Lonsdale. The road sits on a limestone shelf where the water from Gragareth above meets the permeable limestone and disappears back underground. There are kilometres of caves and passages below your feet. For full details you can pick up a caving guidebook.

Rowten Pot is stunning and right on Turbary Road; there is a cave system behind it that's safe to explore.

Yordas Gill scramble.

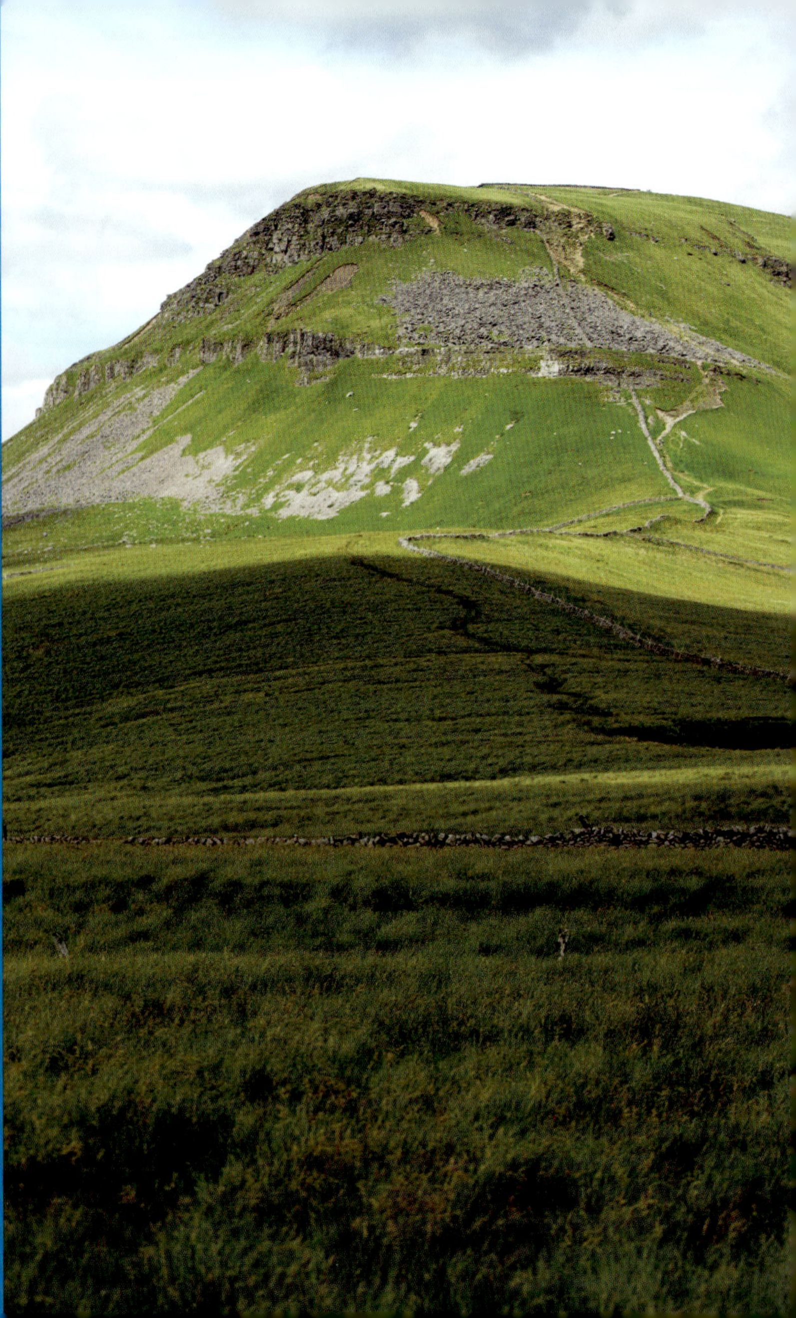

10.2km / 6.3 miles

07 / PEN-Y-GHENT FROM HORTON IN RIBBLESDALE

A classic round and a great introduction to the Three Peaks.

/ ESSENTIAL INFO
GRADE ●●○○
DISTANCE **10.2KM/6.3 MILES**
ASCENT **440M**
TIME **2.5–4 HRS (WALKER)/1.25–2 HRS (RUNNER)**
START/FINISH **HORTON IN RIBBLESDALE YDNP PAY & DISPLAY CAR PARK**
START GRID REF **SD 807 725**
START GPS **54.1489, -2.2961**
OS MAP **OL2 YORKSHIRE DALES: SOUTHERN & WESTERN AREAS (1:25,000)**

/ OVERVIEW
Pen-y-ghent is often the first of the Three Peaks that people try, and rightly so. This short but cracking round is a great introduction to the area. A climb out of Horton in Ribblesdale is topped off by a scramble up the rock steps right on the nose of the hill. It's then a descent along the Pennine Way with visits to Hunt and Hull pots on the way.

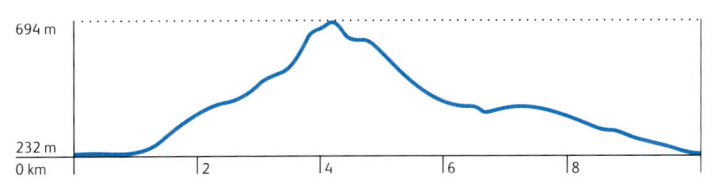

The nose of Pen-y-ghent. © John Coefield

Horton Scar Lane. © Hannah Collingridge

/ DIRECTIONS

S **Turn right** out of the car park and head through the village. Just before St Oswald's church **turn left** on to a paved footpath along the side of a field. It passes through some buildings and comes out on to a minor road; **turn left** and then **turn right** across a bridge to meet a lane. **Turn left** and follow the lane towards Brackenbottom as it climbs and starts to curve back round on itself.

2 Just before the farm buildings take the footpath on the **left** – the gate here may be open or closed; just leave it as you found it. Then use the **middle gate of the three ahead of you** on to more open fellside – the farmer will have clearly marked which is the correct gate to use. The path then climbs pretty much parallel to the wall for about 2km. Particularly sensitive areas suffering from erosion will be fenced off and walkers encouraged to keep to the path; these areas may vary according to the particular erosion controls at any one time. There are a couple of slightly more technical sections up small limestone scars which mark the previous course of water which now runs underground – these would have been little waterfalls in their day. After a couple of frankly unnecessary dips, the path meets a wall and the Pennine Way.

3 **Turn left** on to the Pennine Way and start climbing more steeply. Most of this next section is paved but there are two steeper sections where you will be walking on the bedrock. The second step is the trickier one and you will probably end up using your hands for this part; if you have found the first rock step to be on the edge of your comfort zone, you will probably find the second one even more testing. It is only a short section though. After the second rock

07/PEN-Y-GHENT FROM HORTON IN RIBBLESDALE 37

The second step on Pen-y-ghent. © Hannah Collingridge

step it's a matter of following the flagged path rising gently to the summit and the trig point on Pen-y-ghent. There's a great shelter built in the curve of the wall, and if that's full it's usually possible to find shelter and shade along the wall itself.

4 At the summit there is a signpost clearly directing you down the *Pennine Way* and the *Three Peaks* route **through a wall down a wide path**. It starts off a bit loose but then becomes paved steps before becoming rougher again. It is very clear to follow. There is a sharp bend to the left (signposted) just as you reach the impressive limestone cliffs. Continue downhill. (After a gate you can **bear left** along a narrow grassy trod to a stream and Hunt Pot, a large pothole. Luckily, if you don't fancy the caving, the stream heading into the pothole is spectacular enough. Rejoin the main path via another grassy trod.) Continue **straight ahead** to the path junction at Tarn Bar (SD 822 742). **Turn right** on to a bridleway for 300m then **bear left** to visit Hull Pot.

5 **Retrace your steps** to the junction and continue **straight ahead** along Horton Scar Lane (a typical Dales walled track); the going is varied underfoot. (It's worth having a good look at the dry valley on the left-hand side of the track where a river once ran.) **Bear right** to emerge at the main road. **Turn right** along the main road to return to the car park.

GOOD TO KNOW

PUBLIC TRANSPORT AND ACCESS

Horton in Ribblesdale is on the Settle–Carlisle Railway. DalesBus 11 runs from Settle to Horton.

There is a national park car park with toilets in Horton, plus extra parking at the northern end of the village in a field.

WHEN TO WALK IT

All of the paths are well made so there are very few, if any, muddy sections. The paths can hold puddles after rain. Hull and Hunt pots are even more spectacular after a great deal of rain.

TERRAIN AND NAVIGATION

Mostly well-maintained footpaths and tracks. Some hands-on scrambling needed up the rock steps of Pen-y-ghent for a short distance. All the paths are very clear and well signposted.

FACILITIES AND REFRESHMENTS

There are toilets in the national park car park in Horton. There are pubs in the village and a shop selling refreshments – check opening hours if it's out of season.

Hull Pot. © Hannah Collingridge

DOGS AND KIDS

Livestock and ground-nesting birds mean Pen-y-ghent is a dog-on-lead kind of place, particularly between 1 March and 31 July when it is the law under the CRoW Act that dogs must be on short leads. Dogs with long legs should manage the scrambling; dogs with short legs may need help – ditto for children.

POINTS OF INTEREST

Climbing up through the layers of limestone and sandstone on the nose of Pen-y-ghent is a great way of viewing the changing geology that makes up the Three Peaks.

There are great views on the way up Pen-y-ghent of Fountains Fell and Darnbrook Fell. Fountains is so called because it was owned by Fountains Abbey. Before the Reformation, much of the land round here was held by various monasteries for sheep farming.

The potholes of Hunt and Hull pots are both fascinating to see. At Hull Pot, the stream usually sinks before the pot itself and enters towards the bottom of the hole. In flood conditions the stream pours over the lip of the pot. In extreme conditions the pot itself floods, but that is a pretty rare occurrence and likely to make the news. You can follow the stream bed up to discover where the water is sinking today. It's always a little bit eerie looking at a stream flowing along the bed and just gradually disappearing underground.

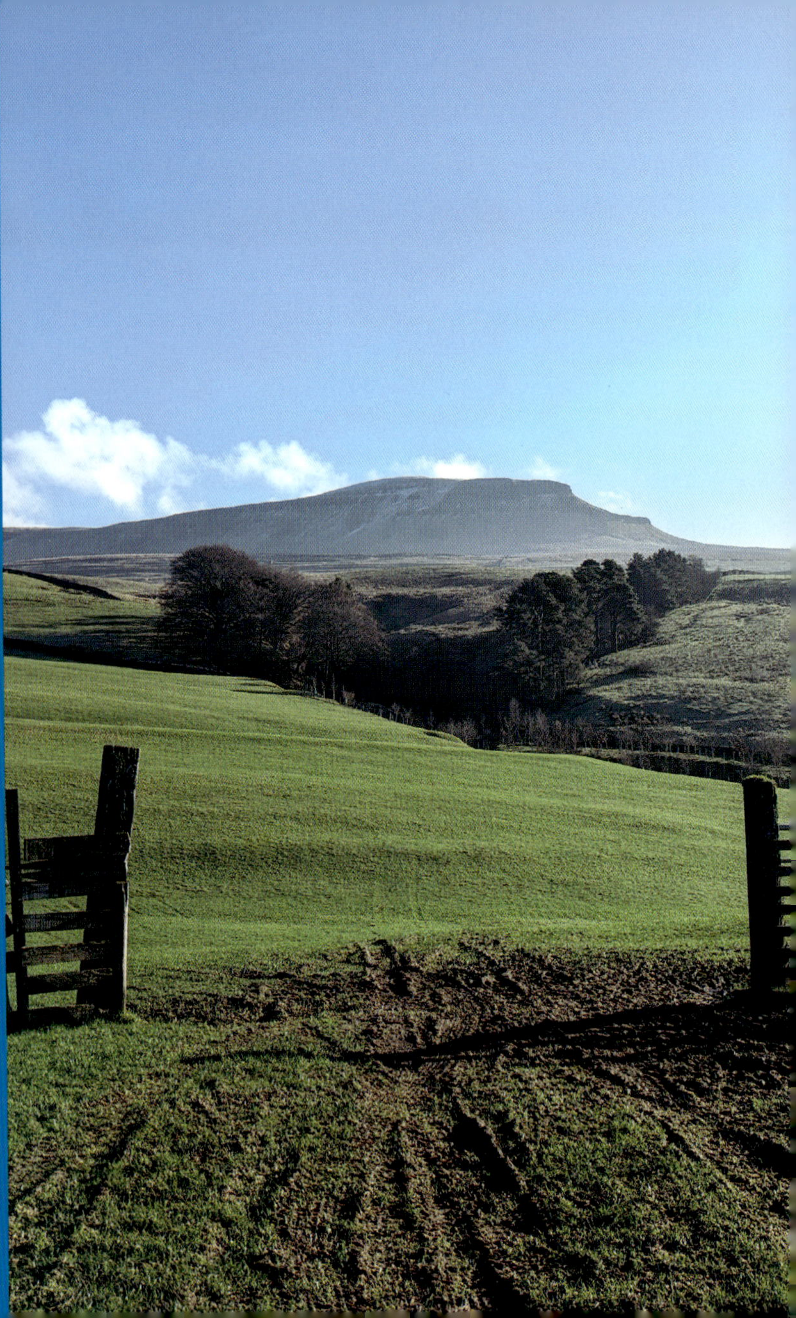

13.6km / 8.5 miles

08 / PEN-Y-GHENT & PLOVER HILL

An extension to walk 7 with a taste of wilder, rougher walking.

/ ESSENTIAL INFO
GRADE ●●○○○
DISTANCE **13.6KM/8.5 MILES**
ASCENT **500M**
TIME **3–5 HRS (WALKER)/2–3 HRS (RUNNER)**
START/FINISH **HORTON IN RIBBLESDALE YDNP PAY & DISPLAY CAR PARK**
START GRID REF **SD 807 725**
START GPS **54.1489, -2.2961**
OS MAP **OL2 YORKSHIRE DALES: SOUTHERN & WESTERN AREAS (1:25,000)**

/ OVERVIEW
While walk 7 is an absolute cracker, this is a great variation giving a rather different perspective on Pen-y-ghent. The walking is certainly more off the beaten track and will almost certainly include boggy sections, but will also give you entirely different views and be very much quieter after the top of Pen-y-ghent.

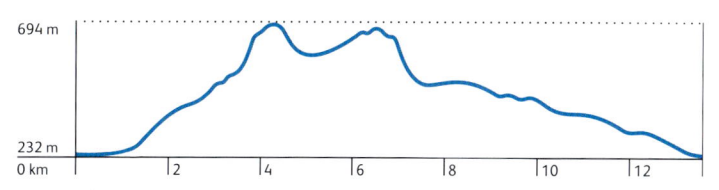

Pen-y-ghent from Horton. © Sarah Lister

/ DIRECTIONS

S **Turn right** out of the car park and head through the village. Just before St Oswald's church **turn left** on to a paved footpath along the side of a field. It passes through some buildings and comes out on to a minor road; **turn left** and then **turn right** across a bridge to meet a lane. **Turn left** and follow the lane towards Brackenbottom as it climbs and starts to curve back round on itself.

2 Just before the farm buildings take the footpath on the **left** – the gate here may be open or closed; just leave it as you found it. Then use the **middle gate of the three ahead of you** on to more open fellside – the farmer will have clearly marked which is the correct gate to use. The path then climbs pretty much parallel to the wall for about 2km. Particularly sensitive areas suffering from erosion will be fenced off and walkers encouraged to keep to the path; these areas may vary according to the particular erosion controls at any one time. There are a couple of slightly more technical sections up small limestone scars which mark the previous course of water which now runs underground – these would have been little waterfalls in their day. After a couple of frankly unnecessary dips, the path meets a wall and the Pennine Way.

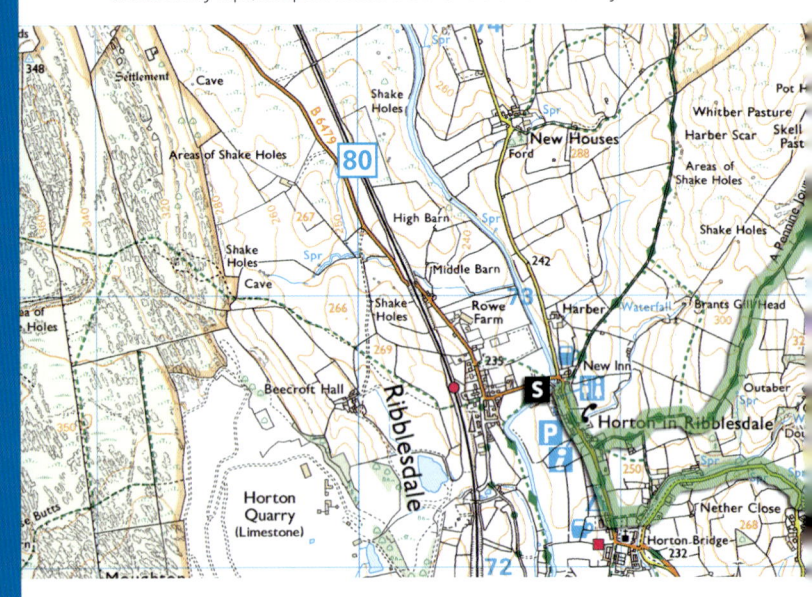

08 / PEN-Y-GHENT & PLOVER HILL   43

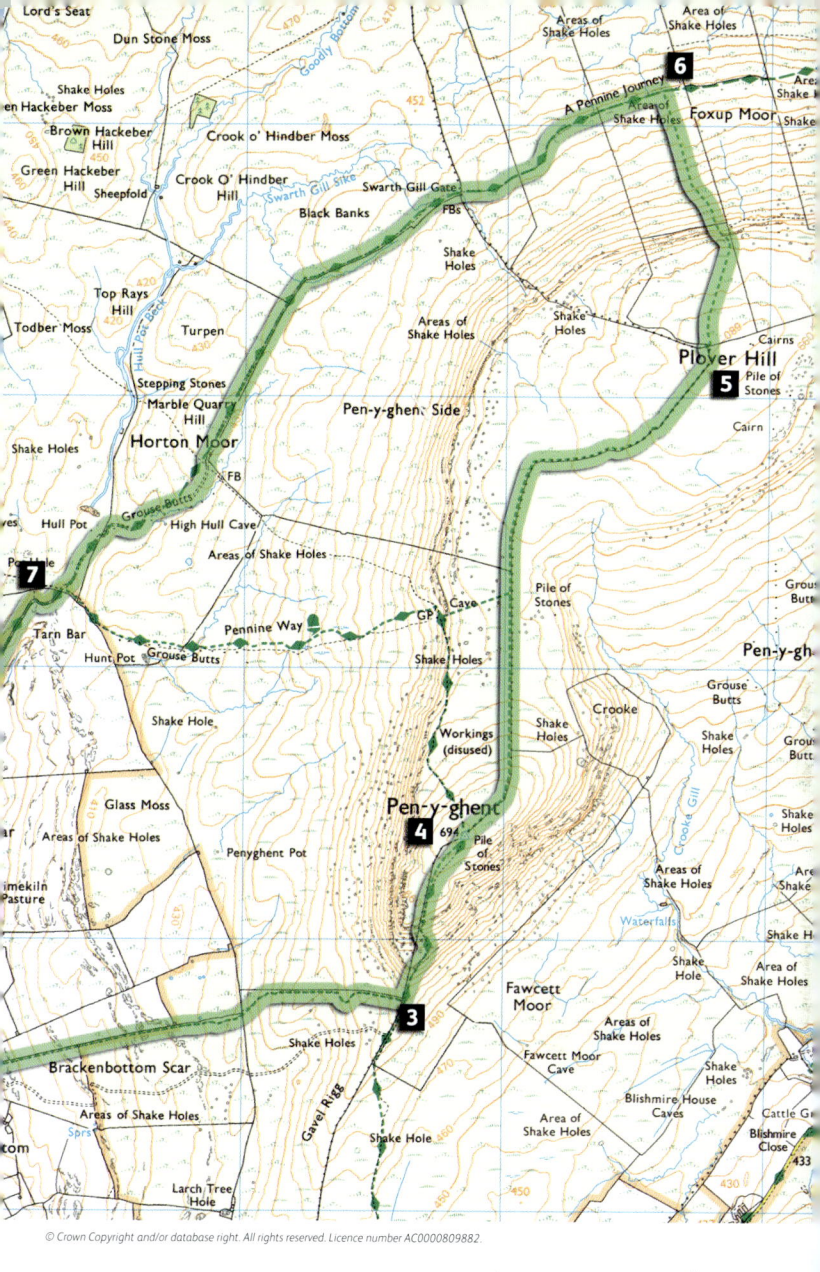

3 **Turn left** on to the Pennine Way and start climbing more steeply. Most of this next section is paved but there are two steeper sections where you will be walking on the bedrock. The second step is the trickier one and you will probably end up using your hands for this part; if you have found the first rock step to be on the edge of your comfort zone, you will probably find the second one even more testing. It is only a short section though. After the second rock step it's a matter of following the flagged path rising gently to the summit and the trig point on Pen-y-ghent. There's a great shelter built in the curve of the wall, and if that's full it's usually possible to find shelter and shade along the wall itself.

4 From the summit, **cross the wall** but instead of following the big path **take the lesser trodden way next to the wall**. Almost immediately the terrain becomes wetter, and you will discover a new appreciation for the team who look after the main Three Peaks footpaths and float them over the soggy ground. The path descends, still parallel to the wall, and continues across varyingly boggy ground. **Cross another wall at right angles to the one you're following via a stile** and continue to run parallel to the original wall as it swings eastwards and rises to the top of Plover Hill. Test your skill and ingenuity as you try to keep your feet dry – whichever variant of the path you are on, another will look drier. You will arrive at a stile in the corner of the wall near the summit of Plover Hill (SD 847 751).

5 From here leave the wall and join the path leading **northwards**. This starts to drop and thankfully is drier than the way up Plover Hill. There's a stepped bit through the steepest, slightly craggy bit and then the path descends to meet the bridleway known as Foxup Road. There's quite a different feel to this side of the hill, and far fewer people.

6 **Turn left** and walk along this old monastic road. The couple of streams you cross will end up in Hull Pot either over or underground. The views of this side of Pen-y-ghent are good, too, and different to the more usual aspect. The old road is easy to follow and brings you to a wall very close to Hull Pot – it's well worth going to have a closer look. After exploring around Hull Pot, pick up the old road again to reach a path junction at Tarn Bar (SD 822 742).

7 Go **straight ahead** along Horton Scar Lane (a typical Dales walled track); the going is varied underfoot. (It's worth having a good look at the dry valley on the left-hand side of the track where a river once ran.) **Bear right** to emerge at the main road. **Turn right** along the main road to return to the car park.

GOOD TO KNOW

PUBLIC TRANSPORT AND ACCESS

Horton in Ribblesdale is on the Settle–Carlisle Railway. DalesBus 11 runs from Settle to Horton.

There is a national park car park with toilets in Horton, plus extra parking at the northern end of the village in a field.

WHEN TO WALK IT

The paths after the top of Pen-y-ghent are likely to be boggy, especially after a wet spell. Hull Pot and the waterfalls on the side of Pen-y-ghent are even more spectacular after a great deal of rain.

TERRAIN AND NAVIGATION

Well-maintained footpaths and tracks while on the Three Peaks route and the Pennine Way. Off these sections you'll need to feel comfortable about choosing a route over boggy ground. In clag, some of these paths are not easy to spot and follow but there are handy walls to aid navigation.

FACILITIES AND REFRESHMENTS

There are toilets in the national park car park in Horton. There are pubs in the village and a shop selling refreshments – check opening hours if it's out of season.

Signage on top of Pen-y-ghent. © Hannah Collingridge

DOGS AND KIDS

Livestock and ground-nesting birds mean Pen-y-ghent is a dog-on-lead kind of place, particularly between 1 March and 31 July when it is the law under the CRoW Act that dogs must be on short leads. Dogs with long legs should manage the scrambling and the bogs; dogs with short legs may need help – ditto for children.

POINTS OF INTEREST

You get the great chance to see the changing layers of limestone and sandstone of Pen-y-ghent in front on your nose on the sharp end of the hill. Walking over Plover Hill towards Foxup gives you not only completely different views but a chance to walk on the old monastic road between Horton and Foxup, now a bridleway.

The pothole Hull Pot is well worth seeing; wandering upstream to find where the water is currently sinking is also interesting, and is usually a good place for a paddle on a hot day.

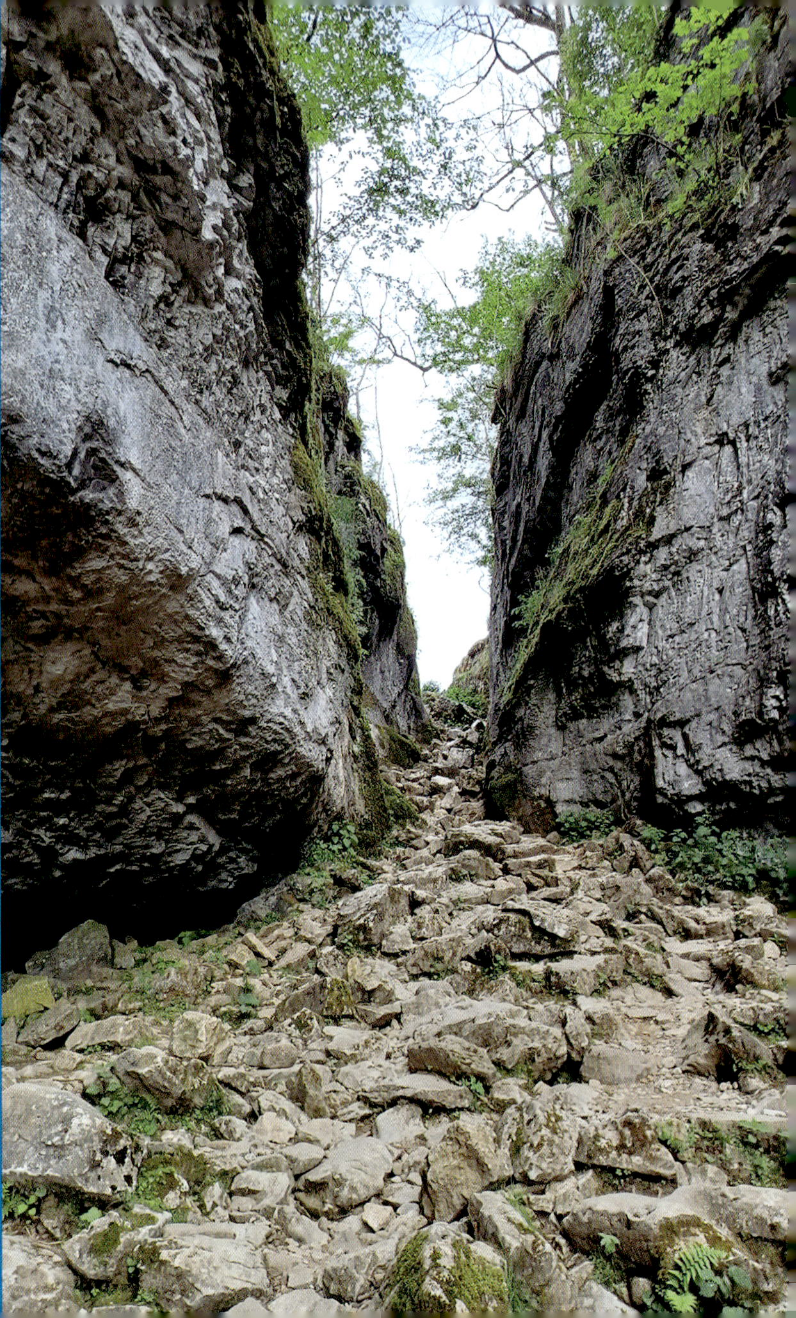

16.6km / 10.3 miles

09 / INGLEBOROUGH FROM CLAPHAM

A great round incorporating the very best parts of this iconic hill in one walk.

/ ESSENTIAL INFO
GRADE ●●●○
DISTANCE **16.6KM/10.3 MILES**
ASCENT **650M**
TIME **3–6 HRS (WALKER)/2–3 HRS (RUNNER)**
START/FINISH **CLAPHAM**
START GRID REF **SD 745 691**
START GPS **54.1171, -2.3915**
OS MAP **OL2 YORKSHIRE DALES: SOUTHERN & WESTERN AREAS (1:25,000)**

/ OVERVIEW
A fairly steady ascent past Ingleborough Cave and through Trow Gill, with a diversion to Gaping Gill, shows off the amazing limestone scenery around the lower levels of the hill. It's then a bit steeper up to Little Ingleborough, before heading below the remains of the hill fort and on to the summit plateau with its fabulous views. The descent starts steeply but soon mellows out, taking you under the flanks of Simon Fell before cutting across on a delightful grassy track towards the Pennine Bridleway and back down to the village.

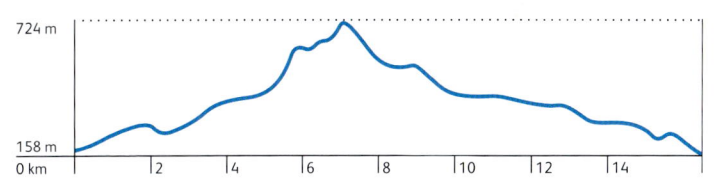

Trow Gill. © Hannah Collingridge

The Gaping Gill winch. © Hannah Collingridge

/ DIRECTIONS

S From the YDNP car park **turn right** up through the village towards the church – you can either cross the river opposite the car park or further up near the church; it matters not as they rejoin on Riverside. Continue up to The Old Sawmill cafe where it's decision time: you can pay an admission charge to go through the grounds of Ingleborough Hall or use the bridleway to the west to get to Ingleborough Cave (see map) – this way gains, and then loses, a little bit more height. To use the nature trail of the hall, pay your admission (card payments accepted) and follow the easy gravel trail through the woods, rejoining the main route at point 2. There are various noticeboards along the way explaining some of the features of this constructed landscape. Or keep going past the cafe to the crossroads and **turn right** up the private road signposted to *Ingleborough Cave*, *Gaping Gill* and *Ingleborough*. Keep **straight ahead** on the track to the farm, through the farm buildings, clearly signed, and then drop down to the well-surfaced track which emerges from the private grounds of the hall. **Turn left** and continue to the show cave.

2 The track continues past the show cave, bends round to the left and enters the gorge of Trow Gill. This stunning gorge was cut by meltwater towards the end of the last ice age. There's now some fairly extreme sport climbing up its walls. The path becomes rockier and picks a way through to the top of the gill past fascinating limestone walls. At the top of Trow Gill you emerge on to more open moorland. The rock underfoot changes from limestone to sandstone and back – you are right on the border between the two layers. Follow the track alongside the wall until you cross it on the **left** using two swing gates/stiles. For a short while the track becomes a little less distinct but continue **straight ahead** and it re-emerges clearly. Where the path splits, take the **right-hand path** to go and see Gaping Gill, one of the most famous potholes in the UK.

09/INGLEBOROUGH FROM CLAPHAM | 49

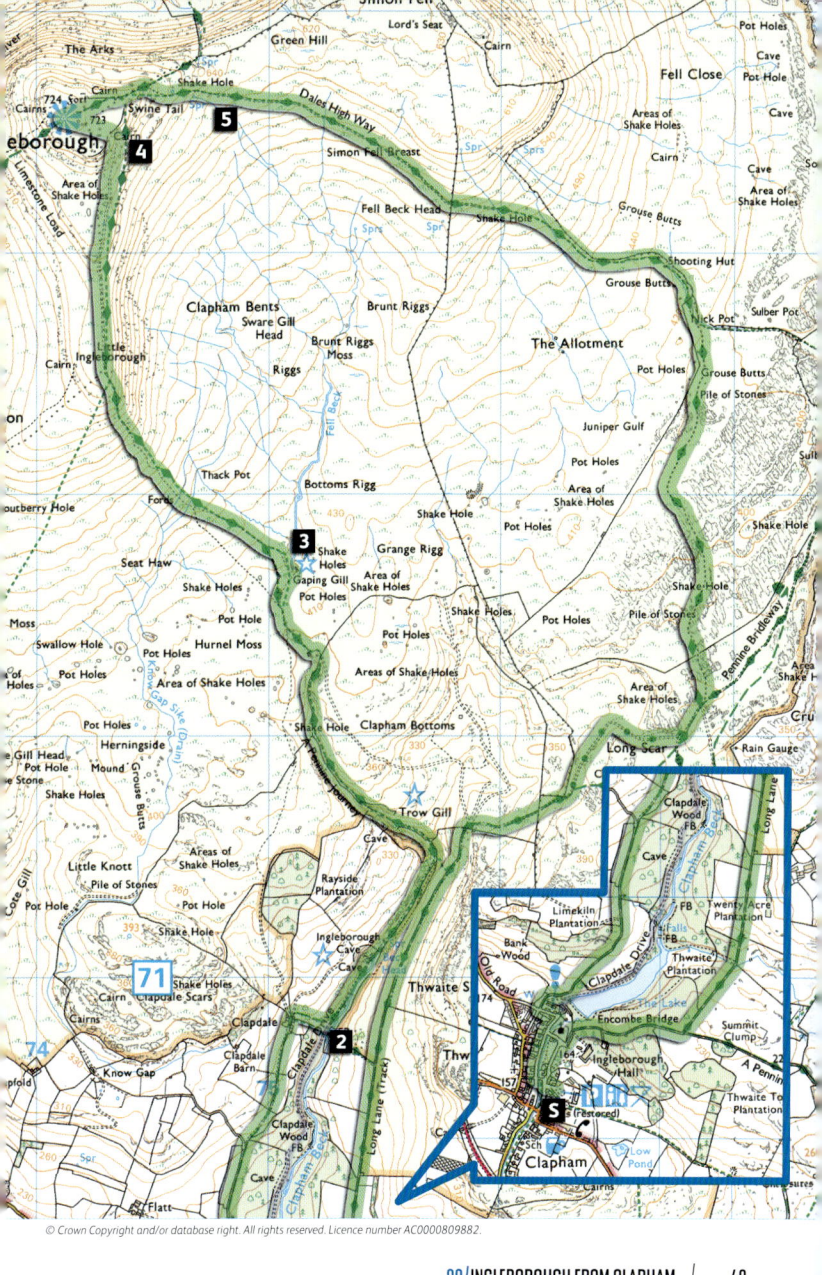

3 Retrace your steps to pick up the path that continues up the hill which then joins the one you ignored at the earlier split. Continue upwards on the clear path but be aware that the rise you can see in front of you is Little Ingleborough – there is another chunk of climbing to do before the summit of Ingleborough is reached. On a clear day you'll be able to see the remnants of the hill fort as you climb up the last bit.

4 The summit is a large plateau and this is where most navigational mistakes are made, especially in mist, as apart from the trig point itself it's surprisingly featureless and the paths off the summit are not altogether clear until you are on them. There are three deliberate, pathed ways off the summit. One is the path from Clapham we have just used in ascent; one goes south-west to Ingleton; and the other leads north-east off the plateau before splitting for Chapel-le-Dale and Horton in Ribblesdale. **This is the path you need to make the round back to Clapham.** Head to the **north-east** corner of the summit plateau where you will descend a steep, natural, rocky staircase and come to a junction of paths: this is sometimes marked by a sign and sometimes it has gone missing – the junction will be clear either way. **Head right** at the junction. You should now be heading east. If you are not, you are on the wrong path.

5 Continue down the obvious path across the southern flank of Simon Fell. As you drop off the limestone there is a spring to the right-hand side of the path. Not only is it delicious water straight from the hillside, but this water will run into Gaping Gill and then through to Ingleborough Cave. Just after an old shooting hut and the second gate there is a split in the path: the main path continues left to Horton on the Three Peaks route, but **bear right** here along a lovely grassy track leading through the limestone pavement to join the Pennine Bridleway. **Turn right** and keep to the track. After a couple of gates there is a footpath on the right that drops back down to the track from the outward route near Trow Gill. If the weather is inclement or really hot, using this path and returning through Ingleborough Hall estate is more sheltered. Otherwise, continue **straight ahead** on Long Lane, a walled limestone track leading back to Clapham. Eventually Long Lane dips down, cruelly adds in some entirely unnecessary uphill and meets Thwaite Lane. **Turn right** and follow the track down to the village.

GOOD TO KNOW

PUBLIC TRANSPORT AND ACCESS

Clapham Station is 3km south-west of the village with frequent trains to and from Leeds. Craven Connection bus 581 connects Clapham along the A65 route between Kirkby Lonsdale and Settle.

There is a national park car park with toilets in Clapham, plus some extra parking around the village. All parking gets very busy at weekends and during the summer.

WHEN TO WALK IT

The paths are all pretty weatherproof and well-draining – there will be some mud on the moor around Gaping Gill after rain and in winter. Obviously clear weather will give the better views.

TERRAIN AND NAVIGATION

The paths are all clear and well-marked except for a short section near Gaping Gill which is a little less clear. The only really tricky piece of navigation is ensuring that the correct path is taken off Ingleborough, especially in mist or low cloud; take a map and compass, and know how to use them.

Inside Gaping Gill's main chamber. © Hannah Collingridge

FACILITIES AND REFRESHMENTS

Toilets in the car park. There's a cracking little village shop which sells many things to eat. Cafes and pubs in the village, too.

DOGS AND KIDS

Livestock and ground-nesting birds mean Ingleborough is a dog-on-lead kind of place, particularly between 1 March and 31 July when it is the law under the CRoW Act that dogs must be on short leads.

As long as they don't fall down any potholes, there is nothing especially dangerous about this walk and it is eminently escapable at most points by simply turning back, so it can be a good – and fun – choice for fit and adventurous youngsters. A shorter, but still exciting, option would be to walk up to Gaping Gill and then reverse the walk.

POINTS OF INTEREST

Ingleborough show cave is bang on the route, and you then climb through Trow Gill, cut by a torrent of meltwater through the limestone. Gaping Gill looks like many another pothole from the surface, but the stream descends about 100m into a huge cavern. There are winch days run by local caving clubs in May and August around the bank holidays which allow non-potholers to descend, and reascend, safely. An amazing trip.

On top of Ingleborough are the remains of a pre-Roman British fort with remnants of buildings.

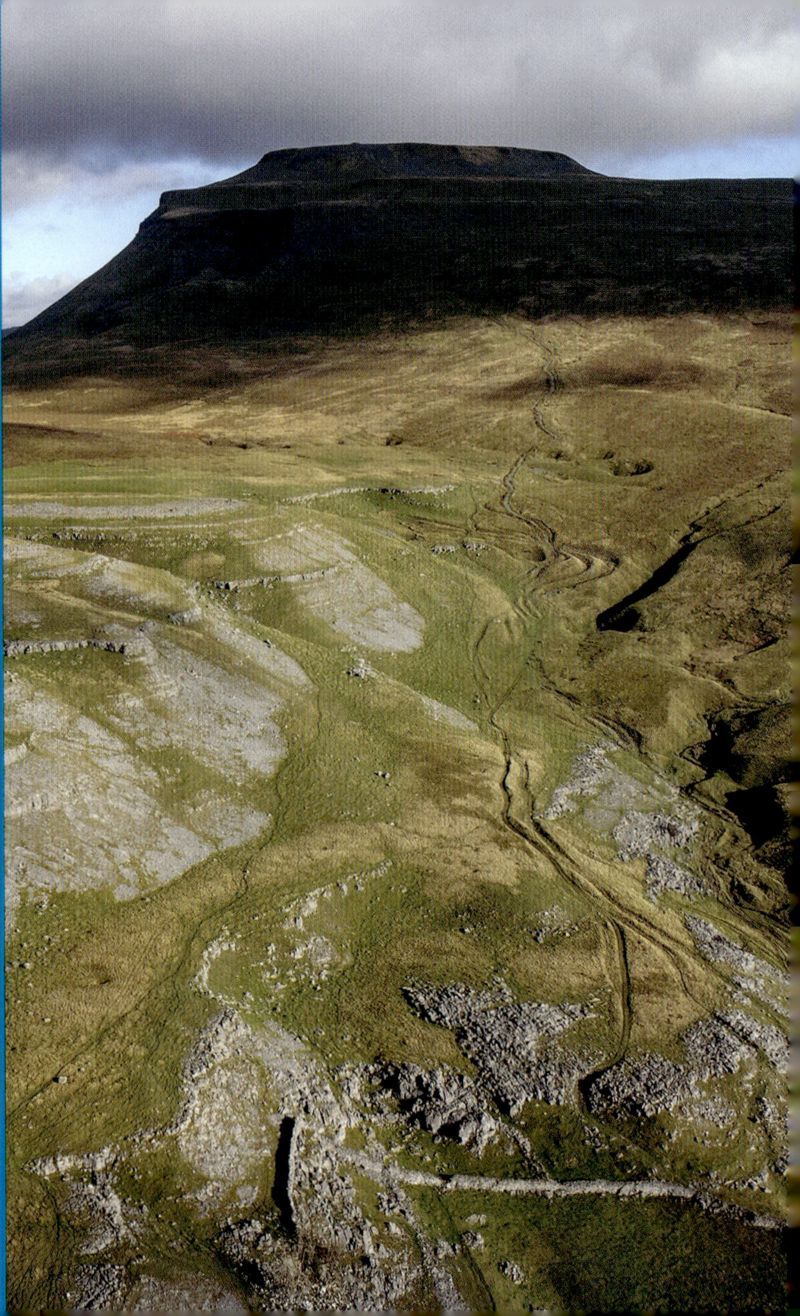

14.3km / 8.9 miles

10 / INGLEBOROUGH FROM INGLETON

Ingleborough directly from the town named after it because it would be rude not to.

/ ESSENTIAL INFO
GRADE ●●●○
DISTANCE **14.3KM/8.9 MILES (11KM AS A THERE-AND-BACK)**
ASCENT **651M (616M AS A THERE-AND-BACK)**
TIME **3.5– 5.5 HRS (WALKER)/1.5–2.5 HRS (RUNNER)**
START/FINISH **MAIN CAR PARK IN INGLETON**
START GRID REF **SD 695 729**
START GPS **54.1519, -2.4682**
OS MAP **OL2 YORKSHIRE DALES: SOUTHERN & WESTERN AREAS (1:25,000)**

/ OVERVIEW
A visually stunning walk from the town through Crina Bottom followed by an ever-steepening climb up Ingleborough. Then either a simple retracing of footsteps back to town, or an off-piste wander through the limestone pavements of Raven Scar finding your own way and exploring. If going pathless and trusting your own navigation isn't for you, the out-and-back route is more suitable.

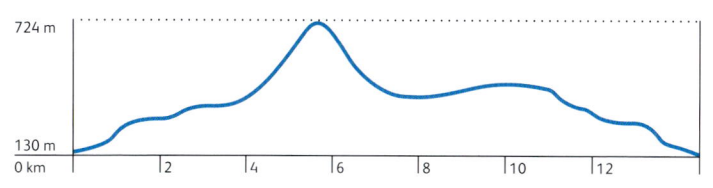

The glacial landscape of Crina Bottom and Ingleborough.

/ DIRECTIONS

S With your back to the community centre in the main car park, **turn left** to the road and then **left** up the road towards Ribblehead and Hawes. The roads bends round to the right, becoming shaded by trees, and the back road to Clapham is on the right. The pavement runs out and there is a short, walled section after which a track leads off to the **right: take this** – it should be signposted as a bridleway to *Ingleborough*. Follow the track which levels out a bit after the initial climb and becomes walled. Go through a gate at SD 719 733 and the track and vistas open out as you enter access land.

2 This is Crina Bottom and a splendid spot it is, too. Continue **straight ahead**, keep **right** at the fork, and follow the rougher track as it starts to climb. It steepens and gets rougher as you leave the limestone but much of the path has been built to help with erosion. There are three steep sections with tantalisingly flatter bits in between before you reach the summit of Ingleborough. The trig point is straight in front of you. The cairns which mark the final section of path can be handy in poor visibility.

3 Decision time. You can retrace your steps back to Ingleton – your path is the one closest to the trig point with those three steep sections and flatter bits in between. Otherwise our main route heads to the north-eastern corner of the plateau and takes the path towards Chapel-le-Dale. This starts with a series of natural rock steps. **Keep left** at the fork and descend on a flagged path to a spring and a gate. This is a great place to pick up water if you are running low.

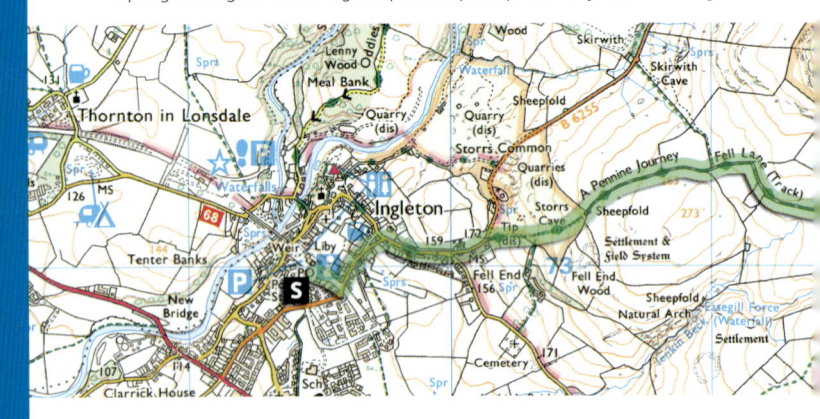

54 | MOUNTAIN WALKS **YORKSHIRE THREE PEAKS**

10/INGLEBOROUGH FROM INGLETON   55

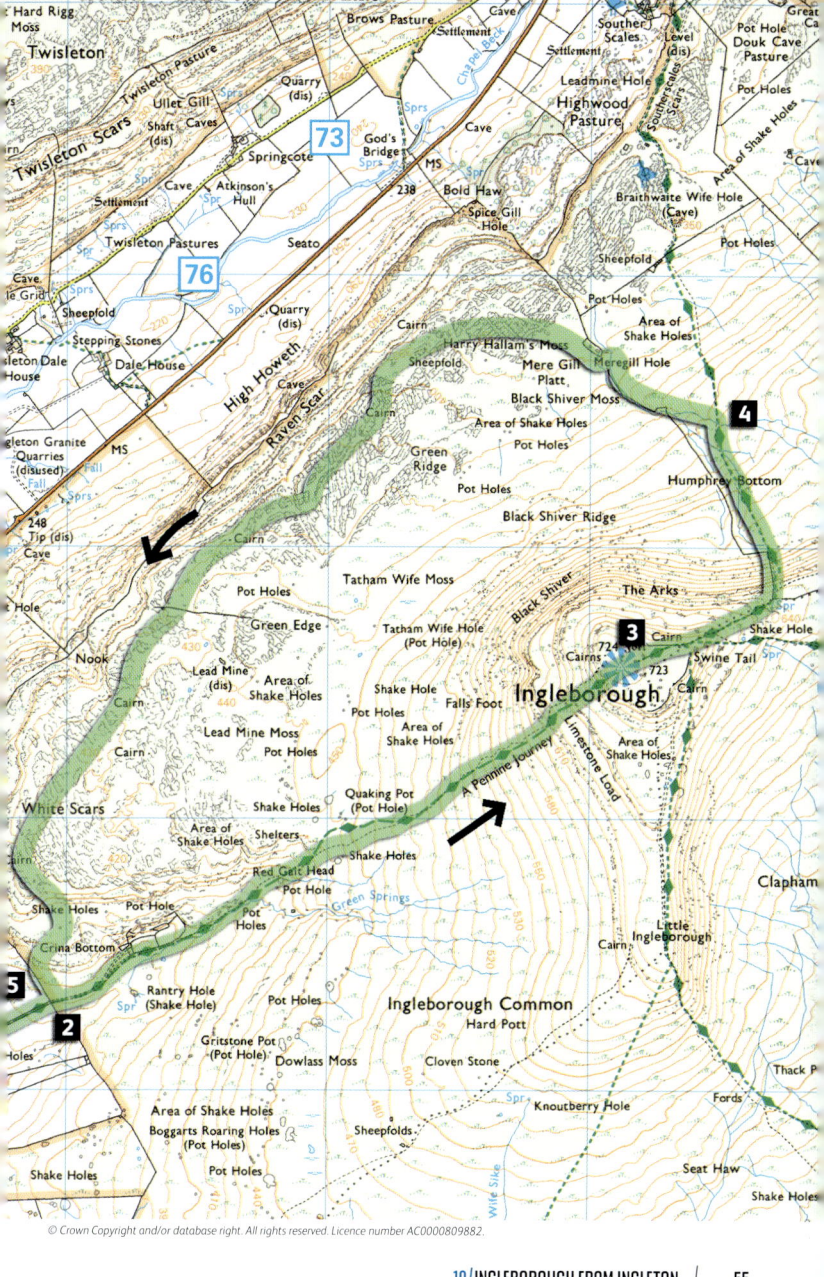

Ingleborough from Fell Lane.

Go through the gate and keep to the made path which steeply descends a stone staircase. This is not a great place for vertigo sufferers. The path then becomes flagged again and much less steep. You will start to cross streams. One has a bridge of three huge flags and the next descends into a little gully. As you climb out of the gully look for a faint path on the **left**.

4 **Follow this faint path**, keeping roughly parallel with the wall and stream to cross a stile in the wall around SD 740 757 which takes you to Meregill Hole. This is yet another entrance into a huge cave system below ground. We're on the same side of Ingleborough as the show cave of White Scar, and the whole fellside is riddled with underground systems. On the horizon to the west there is a large cairn – make your way there any way you choose, admiring the limestone pavements as you probably pass Harry Hallam's sheepfold. At times there are helpful sheep trods, at other times they go in completely the wrong direction. From the large cairn the idea is to make your way along the scars in a south-westerly direction – there is a series of cairns which will help with general direction. You may or may not come across a larger grassy path which leads nicely back down to the gate at SD 719 733. If not, make your way to the **right** of the lone tree and pick your way down. It's one of those walks where you'll never pick the same line twice, but every time you'll have a lovely quiet walk through stunning scenery.

5 Once back at the gate, retrace your steps down to the village. On a good day the views of the Lake District and Morecambe Bay are stunning. Impress your friends by telling them that the prominent triangular hill in the Lakes is Caw.

GOOD TO KNOW

PUBLIC TRANSPORT AND ACCESS

Ingleton is connected along the A65 between Kirkby Lonsdale and Settle by Craven Connection bus 581 which stops at the car park. The car park has toilets, a tourist information point, a community centre and a cricket pitch. There's another car park just up the road and sometimes a bit of parking at Storrs Common up the Ribblehead/Hawes road.

WHEN TO WALK IT

The path straight up and down can get wet but not too boggy. The off-piste section can vary from damp to very soggy after a lot of rain, and walking in/on/through limestone pavements is easier in dry conditions.

TERRAIN AND NAVIGATION

This route has straightforward navigation and terrain up the hill on a variety of mostly stony surfaces with some maintained paths and steps. The off-piste section is across rather rough moorland and limestone pavement with the odd sheep track – it's not the easiest and quickest surface to walk on, especially if you aren't used to it.

View down Fell Lane.

There's also the extremely steep path down from Ingleborough to get to the off-piste section.

FACILITIES AND REFRESHMENTS

Toilets in the car park. Plenty of cafes and pubs, and there's a chippy in town. There's also a Co-op.

DOGS AND KIDS

Livestock and ground-nesting birds mean Ingleborough is a dog-on-lead kind of place, particularly between 1 March and 31 July when it is the law under the CRoW Act that dogs must be on short leads.

As long as they don't fall down any grikes or potholes, there is nothing especially dangerous about this walk especially on the there-and-back route, so it can be a good – and fun – choice for fit and adventurous youngsters.

POINTS OF INTEREST

Crina Bottom is a delightful spot with great evidence of glacial action – one half of the valley is scraped clean, the other in the lee of Ingleborough has a dump of till. The differences in vegetation, even just the colour of the grass, between the two sides are striking.

The limestone pavements on Raven Scar are as stunning as the views: ever-changing views of a massive-looking Ingleborough, plus the limestone scars on Twisleton and the bottom end of the Turbary Road. Views of Morecambe Bay and the Lakes on a good day will entertain you on the lane back down.

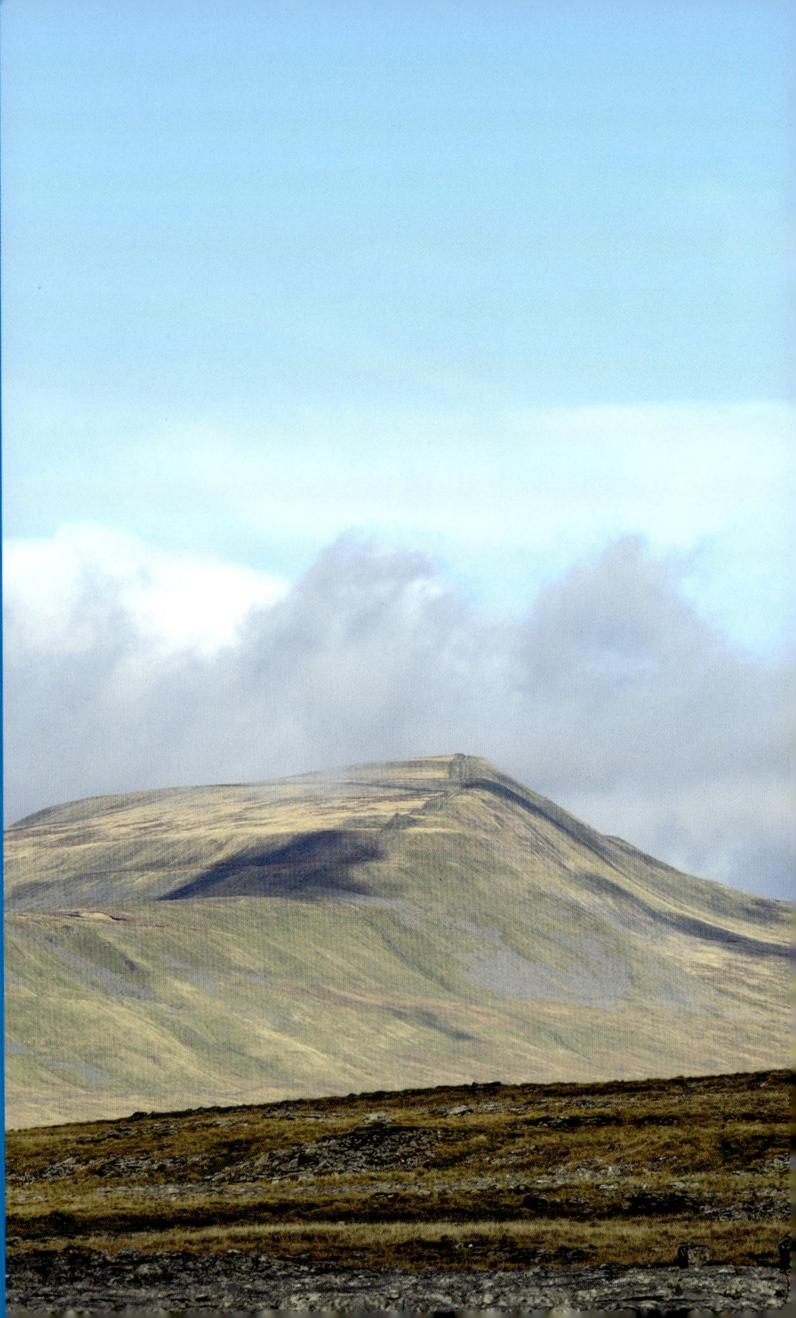

12.7km / 7.9 miles

11 / WHERNSIDE FROM RIBBLEHEAD

A splendid round of Whernside following the Three Peaks route up but cutting back to Ribblehead after the descent.

/ ESSENTIAL INFO
GRADE ●●●○
DISTANCE **12.7KM/7.9 MILES**
ASCENT **490M**
TIME **3–4 HRS (WALKER)/1.5–2.5 HRS (RUNNER)**
START/FINISH **RIBBLEHEAD**
START GRID REF **SD 765 792**
START GPS **54.2089, -2.3611**
OS MAP **OL2 YORKSHIRE DALES: SOUTHERN & WESTERN AREAS (1:25,000)**

/ OVERVIEW
A long, fairly gentle ascent begins by running parallel to the Settle–Carlisle Railway before sweeping round up the broad ridge to the summit of Whernside and glorious views. A steep descent leads to a return to Ribblehead (Batty Moss) viaduct on tracks and through fields. This route can also be started from Ribblehead Station.

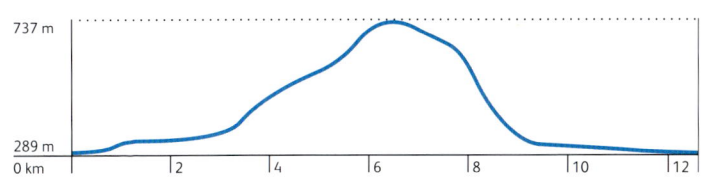

View to Whernside from White Scars.

Ribblehead (Batty Moss) viaduct and distant Pen-y-ghent.

/ DIRECTIONS

S From the T-junction in the road take the signed gravelled path towards the viaduct. This path joins a larger gravelled track – continue towards the viaduct. Where the larger track swings left under the viaduct, continue **straight ahead** on the smaller path parallel to the railway to climb a set of steps. Continue on this clear path with the railway to your left.

2 About 600m after Blea Moor signal box, still a working part of the Settle–Carlisle railway, there is a fork in the path (SD 760 812): **take the left fork** and drop down to cross the river. The path then climbs slightly to cross the railway. From this area the views of Force Gill are excellent. The path starts to steepen as it climbs Slack Hill. The gradient gets a little more gentle and the old road to Dent continues straight on.

3 The path up Whernside clearly leads off on the **left**. It's the obvious path – wider and more maintained than the old road, and signposted over the stile. It's now simply a case of following this path up and round to the top of Whernside. Below you as you ascend is Greensett Tarn in a hollow left by the last glacier. There is a shelter on the summit and the trig point is through the drystone wall. On a clear day the views are stunning and include the other two Three Peaks, the northern Dales and Howgills, plus Morecambe Bay and the Lakes.

11/WHERNSIDE FROM RIBBLEHEAD 61

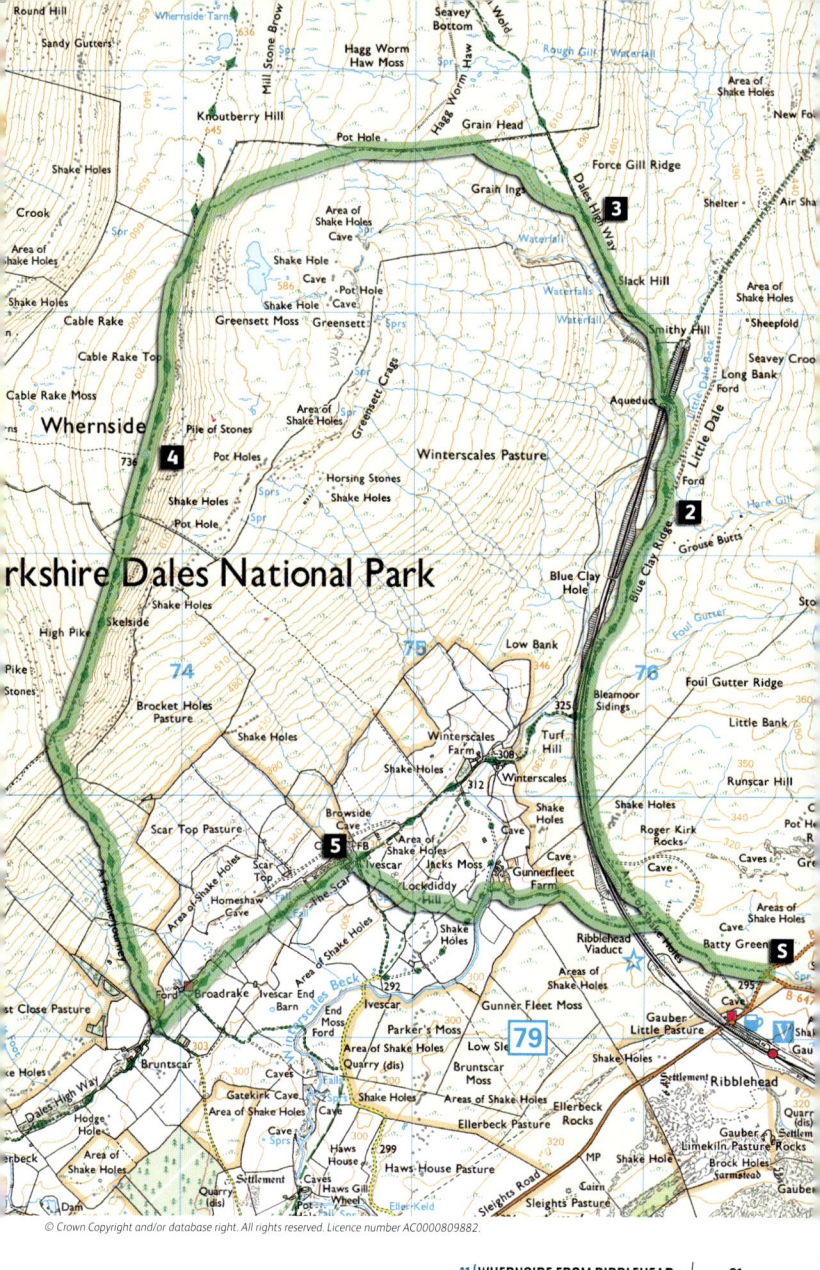

Blea Moor signal box and Ingleborough.

4 From the summit, **continue south** on the broad path down the ridge and then **bear left** down the steep paved and stepped descent. As you pass through a gate the gradient becomes gentler. At the next gate, **turn left** through the gate, signposted as a bridleway to *Winterscales*. After the first field path you come to Broadrake which offers bunk accommodation and a variety of craft activities. **Bear right** through their yard to follow the path. After a very short field and then a longer one you join a gravelled track leading into the farmyard at Ivescar. The scar behind the farm is riddled with caves.

5 **Turn right** at the big junction in the middle of the yard and **then immediately left** after the building over a stile along the signed footpath. Aim **diagonally right** for the corner of the field where there is a stile marked by yellow posts and a flap over the top of the wall. Keep parallel to the wall up and over Lock-diddy Hill, a drumlin, then steeply down to a stile, parallel to the wall to the bottom of the field and then **turn left**. Head diagonally across the sometimes marshy field under the telegraph wires aiming in the direction of the viaduct. After another stile keep to the wall line and join a bigger farm track. **Turn left** and then **right** on the signposted big track, walking under the viaduct, to follow it back to Ribblehead. The viaduct is always there to confirm you are heading in the right direction.

MOUNTAIN WALKS **YORKSHIRE THREE PEAKS**

GOOD TO KNOW

PUBLIC TRANSPORT AND ACCESS

Ribblehead is on the Settle–Carlisle Railway, with trains to Leeds and Carlisle.

There's parking at Ribblehead around the road junction. All parking gets very busy at weekends and during the summer. Please don't drive up to the viaduct as it's a protected site.

WHEN TO WALK IT

This walk is best saved for a day with visibility as the views are far-ranging. If there are southerly winds you will be walking into them up and along the summit ridge – it's possible to reverse the outward route from the summit instead.

TERRAIN AND NAVIGATION

Clear, waymarked, weatherproof paths except for the field return to the viaduct. The main path up the ridge of Whernside is pretty clear, even in low visibility.

FACILITIES AND REFRESHMENTS

The Station Inn at Ribblehead has Portaloos in the car park, plus a water tap, for the use of walkers. They are (at the time of writing) open for food from 12–9 p.m. If you use their facilities, please contribute to their running costs.

DOGS AND KIDS

Livestock and ground-nesting birds mean Whernside is a dog-on-lead kind of place, particularly between 1 March and 31 July when it is the law under the CRoW Act that dogs must be on short leads.

There is nothing inherently hazardous for kids if they can cope with distance and ascent. A shorter option would be to walk up to the railway aqueduct and then reverse the walk.

POINTS OF INTEREST

The iconic Ribblehead – or, technically, Batty Moss – viaduct took five years to build from 1870, with a large workforce who lived on site in shanty towns. The surviving earthworks of these are now a scheduled monument – easiest to spot are the tramways which connected various parts of the construction works. The viaduct was the main bone of contention about the potential closure of the line in the 1980s. British Rail wanted to shut the line, partly because of the costs involved in making structures such as the viaduct safe. The work cost £3 million (in the 1990s), but the line remains open.

You'll pass Blea Moor

The aqueduct over the railway.

signal box en route, the last surviving signal box on this stretch of the Settle–Carlisle railway, and cross over a combined viaduct and aqueduct – a cunning and stunning bit of Victorian engineering – which carries the old road and the stream over the railway just before Blea Moor Tunnel. At nearly a mile and a half long, the tunnel is the longest on the line, and the moor above is marked by clearly visible ventilation shafts and old spoil heaps.

There are great views of the other two Three Peaks from this route, plus you can spot the line of the Roman road heading up Cam Fell to the east.

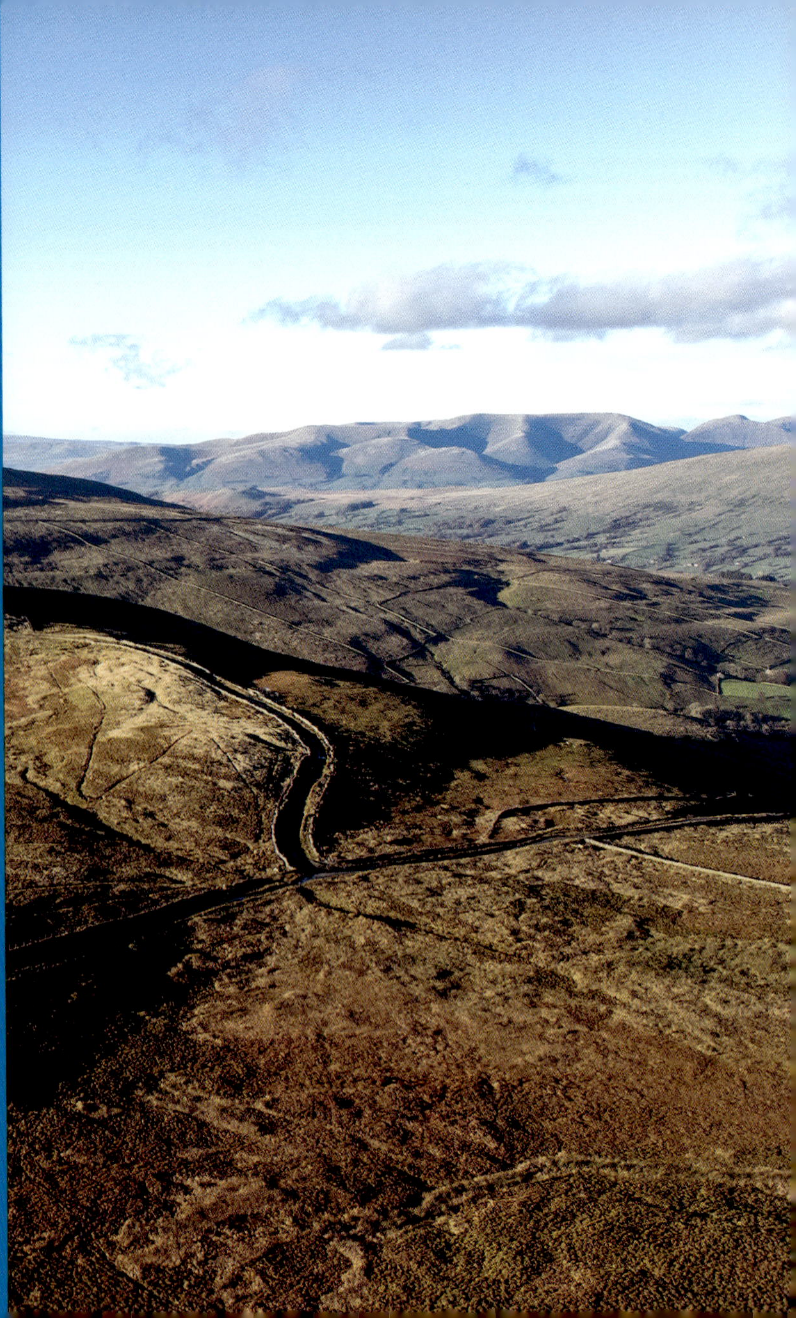

19.3km / 12 miles

12 / WHERNSIDE FROM DENT

A bigger and quieter day out up the largest of the Three Peaks from the picturesque village of Dent.

/ ESSENTIAL INFO
GRADE ●●●○
DISTANCE **19.3KM/12 MILES**
ASCENT **694M**
TIME **4–7 HRS (WALKER)/2–4 HRS (RUNNER)**
START/FINISH **DENT**
START GRID REF **SD 704 870**
START GPS **54.2783, -2.4555**
OS MAP **OL2 YORKSHIRE DALES: SOUTHERN & WESTERN AREAS (1:25,000)**

/ OVERVIEW
Starting from Dent with a steep but interesting ascent of Flinter Gill, this is a longer and wilder walk than many of the others in this book. It's likely to be much quieter than the traditional routes but that also means the paths aren't as well-maintained. Be prepared for a degree of roughness and wetness underfoot. There are great views of the Howgills, geologically closer to the Lakes than the Dales, and the quieter northern Dales.

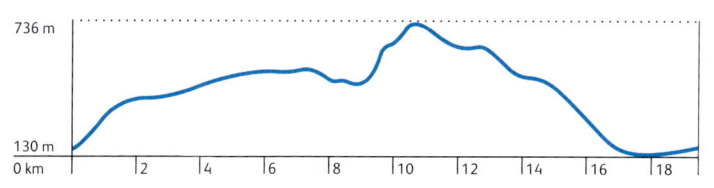

The Occupation Road and the Howgills.

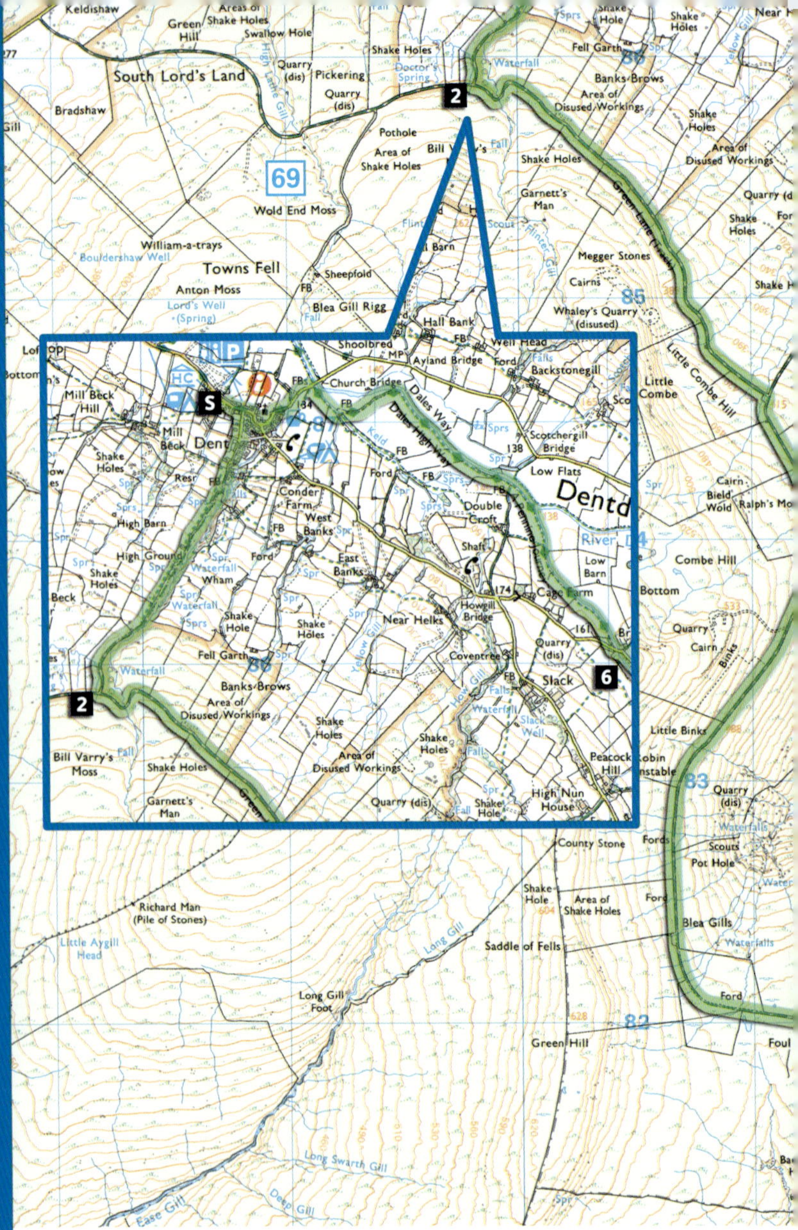
Keldishaw
Green Hill
Areas of Shake Holes
Swallow Hole
South Lord's Land
Bradshaw
High Lathe Gill
Quarry (dis)
Pickering
Quarry (dis)
Shake Holes
Doctor's Spring
2
Pothole
Area of Shake Holes
Bill Varry's
Fall
69
Wold End Moss
William-a-trays
Bouldershaw Well
Towns Fell
Anton Moss
Lord's Well (Spring)
Sheepfold
FB
Blea Gill Rigg
Fell Garth
Banks Brows
Area of Disused Workings
Shake Holes
Area of Disused Workings
Waterfall
Shake Holes
Garnett's Man
Scout
Flinter Gill
Barn
Megger Stones
Cairns
85
Whaley's Quarry (disused)
Green Lane
Quarry (dis)
Shake Holes
Hall Bank
Shoolbred
MP
Ayland Bridge
FB
Well Head
Ford
Backstonegill
Little Combe
Little Combe Hill
Church Bridge
Dales Way
Dales High Way
Mill Beck Hill
HC
S
Mill Beck
Dent
Keld
Shake Holes
Resr
Sprs
Scotchergill Bridge
138
Low Flats
Dentdale
River Dee
High Barn
Conder Farm
West Banks
FB
Ford
Double Croft
Pennine Journey
High Ground
Waterfall
Wham
East Banks
Shaft
Low Barn
Combe Hill
Shake Holes
Beck
174
Cage Farm
Bottom
Waterfall
Shake Hole
Shake Holes
Near Helks
Howgill Bridge
Quarry (dis)
161
Quarry
Cairn
Binks
Yellow Gill
Fell Garth
86
Waterfall
Coventree
How Gill
Falls
FB
Slack
6
Banks Brows
Area of Disused Workings
Waterfall
Slack Well
Little Binks
Shake Holes
Shake Holes
Bill Varry's Moss
Shake Holes
Area of Disused Workings
Fall
Peacock Hill
Robin Constable
83
Quarry (dis)
Garnett's Man
Quarry (dis)
Shake Hole
High Nun House
Spr
County Stone
Fords
Waterfalls
Scouts
Pot Hole
Shake Hole
Area of Shake Holes
Richard Man (Pile of Stones)
Ford
Little Aygill Head
Blea Gills
Long Gill
Saddle of Fells
Waterfalls
Long Gill Foot
Ford
82
Green Hill
Long Swarth Gill
Ease Gill
Deep Gill

12/WHERNSIDE FROM DENT   67

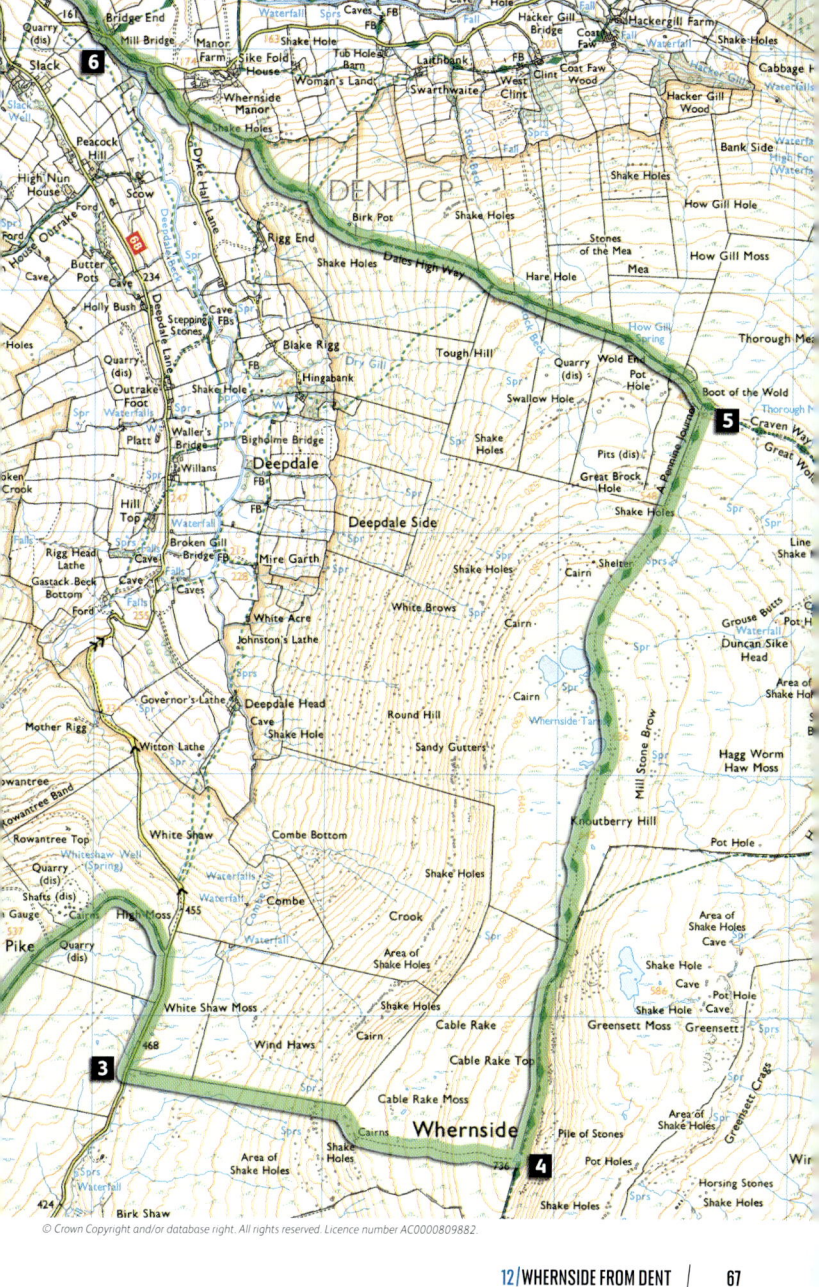

The Adam Sedgwick memorial in Dent.

DIRECTIONS

S Leave the car park, **turn left and then immediately right** following the sign to *Dragon Croft*. More villages should have names like this for their greens. Just past the village green keep **straight ahead**, past the old Zion Chapel, and keep to the **right (straight ahead)**. The tarmac ends and the track immediately becomes steep and rough. Shortly, on the left in the streambed, are some slabs of bedrock previously used for fulling or walking cloth, and now known as the Dancing Flags. There's also a reconstructed lime kiln and the Wishing Tree with splendid roots to distract you from the steep climb on cold legs. At the top of the trail there's a viewpoint and the track emerges on to open land before joining 'Occy' – the Occupation Road between Barbondale and Kingsdale.

2 **Turn left** and follow the walled track as it undulates across the hillside under Great Coum. **Keep right** at the junction with Nun House Outrake. The track is easy to follow but is prone to being wet; it's more of a streambed than a path in places after heavy rain. It gets drier and the surface improves as it swings around the head of Gastack and drops down to the tarmac road. **Turn right** at the road and follow it for 500m, over the crest of the hill, dropping slightly to a stile back on to the access land at SD 721 817. This is clearly marked by both the farmer and YDNP.

The western slope of Whernside.

3 From here follow the path upwards, keeping roughly parallel with the wall. The bottom section is quite soggy but it dries out a bit as the gradient increases. There's a steeper rocky section before the wall heads off to the left. **Keep following the path, not the wall** – there's another boggy section, then another steeper section before the last gentle rise right to the trig point. As you arrive at the top you can usually surprise some of those who have come up from Ribblehead and haven't noticed there's a different way up. There are walled shelters on either side of the main wall. The views from the top are spectacular in good weather.

4 From the trig point go through the wall and **turn left** on to the main ridge path. After 900m look for a stile and path on the left – it is marked as access land, and occurs before the main path starts swinging away to the right, towards the end of Greensett Tarn below you. Take this path **left**; it can be easy to miss if you are relaxing and striding out after the ascent. It's another thin path across more potentially boggy ground which leads past Whernside Tarns, before dropping down to join the old Dent road – if you've ever come up Whernside from Ribblehead it is this track you follow for much of the way. Whernside Tarns is a great spot on a calm day for a bit of a sit.

Whernside from Kingsdale.

5 At the Dent road **turn left** along the track and keep following it. This is an old track, presumably once used by packhorses and traders. At the point we join it it becomes walled and it neatly uses the well-draining shelf of limestone across the hillside. On older maps, a couple of wells are marked along this section which predate the enclosure. The track becomes steeper before emerging on to a small road. **Turn right**, and then **left** at the next junction on to the larger small road.

6 Follow this road until Mill Bridge. Cross the river and **turn right** along a small path running parallel with the beck. This beck joins the River Dee and the path continues to run alongside it. The path then swings away from the river across a field – signed and still fenced – to cross a small beck via a concrete bridge. **Turn right**, waymarked, following the path to the big road bridge. **Turn left** and follow the road through Dent village back to the car park.

GOOD TO KNOW

PUBLIC TRANSPORT AND ACCESS

There is a station called Dent on the Settle–Carlisle Railway. However, it's nearly 8km from the village above Cowgill. As the old joke goes, the answer to the question, 'Why isn't the station nearer the village?' is, 'So it can be on the railway.' There is a connecting DalesBus (Kendal Shuttle S1) from Kendal and Sedbergh to Dent and the station, but it is occasional and seasonal.

There's a car park in the village, which is where the walk begins. All parking gets very busy at weekends and during the summer.

WHEN TO WALK IT

Best saved for a day with visibility as the views are far-ranging. After rain, the Occy (Occupation Road) below Great Coum does become very wet, and the path from Whernside to the old Dent road can also have boggy sections.

TERRAIN AND NAVIGATION

You'll need to be confident on rougher tracks and paths, picking your way up a hillside, and on softer ground. In low cloud some of the paths can be tricky to follow, so good navigation skills are a must. Carry a map and compass and know how to use them.

FACILITIES AND REFRESHMENTS

There are toilets in the car park in Dent. There are several cafes and pubs in Dent itself, plus a small shop. Beware seasonal opening hours.

DOGS AND KIDS

Livestock and ground-nesting birds mean Whernside is a dog-on-lead kind of place. This walk uses paths that are not rights of way across grouse moors so check restrictions on the Natural England website before you go: **www.openaccess.naturalengland.org.uk**

There is nothing inherently hazardous for kids if they can cope with distance, ascent and roughness of terrain.

POINTS OF INTEREST

Flinter Gill is a fascinating start to the walk and the local community has created a trail pointing out things of interest as you ascend. Occupation Road ('Occy') is an old drove road which was walled in 1859 as part of the Inclosure Acts – its very name gives an insight into how it was viewed locally.

The 'Occy'.

Dent is a cracking little village and very picturesque with its cobbled streets and roads so small that modern cars really look out of place. On the way through the village you'll pass the large church of St Andrew's which has been here in various guises since the 12th century, as well as several various non-denominational chapels. Like many isolated places in the north, the varieties of Protestantism in a small area are astounding. There's also a lump of granite remembering early geologist Adam Sedgwick who was born here.

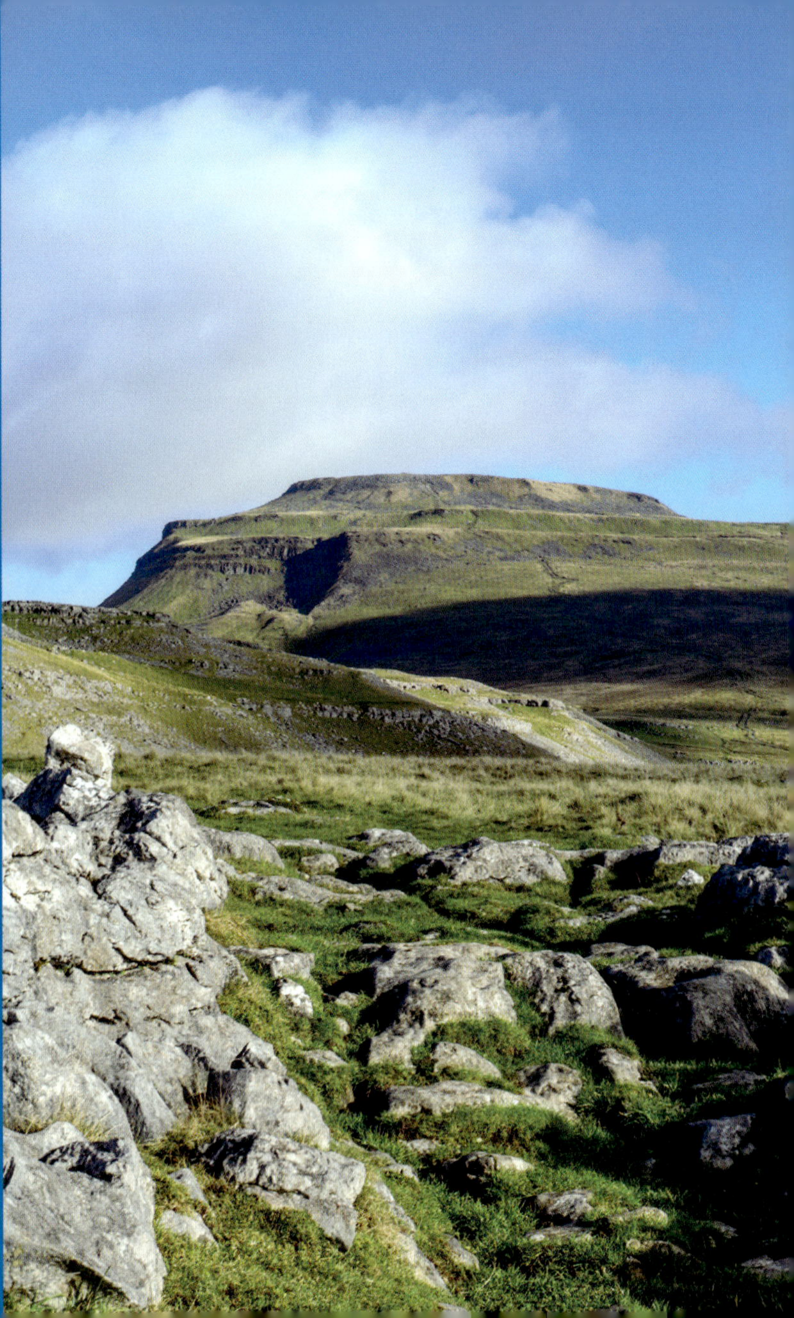

ALL THREE PEAKS IN ONE

Traditionally, the Three Peaks are walked (or run!) anticlockwise from Horton within a 12-hour time limit, but there's no particular reason for that timing, so don't feel obliged to rush. There are three road crossings along the 39-kilometre route which make good start/finish/support points, and these can be used to mix the route up as you wish. These road crossings are:
- B6479 in Horton-in-Ribblesdale
- B6255 at Ribblehead, just north of the Station Inn
- B6255 at Chapel-le-Dale, near the Old Hill Inn

With this in mind, the following pages feature options for either doing the route all in one in a single push, starting where you will and walking anticlockwise (walk 13, page 75) or clockwise (walk 14, page 86), or walking it over two or three days (pages 92–93). The anticlockwise and clockwise directions are split into three sections between the road crossings at Horton, Ribblehead and Chapel-le-Dale – simply refer to the section you are on at the time.

If you fancy upping the challenge, details are also included for what we've called the Super Three Peaks, which instead starts from Ingleton and adds around eight kilometres and 185 metres of ascent to the traditional Three Peaks route. See walk 15, page 95.

Ingleborough from Crina Bottom.

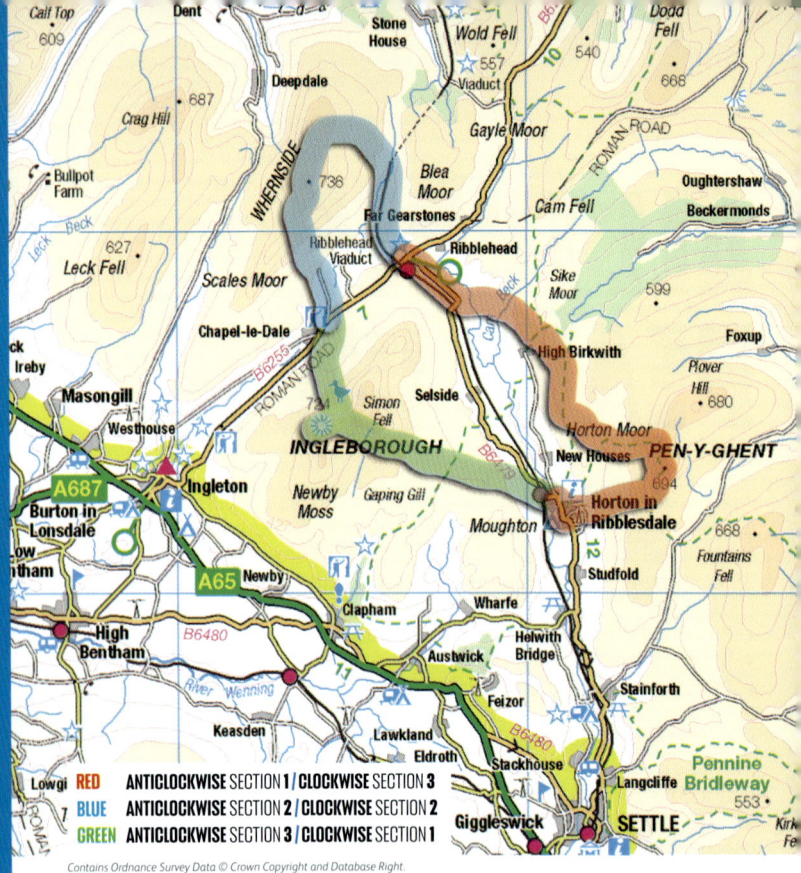

SECTION	START	FINISH	DISTANCE	ASCENT	HILL	MAPS (PAGES)	DIRECTIONS (PAGES)
ANTICLOCKWISE: SECTION 1	HORTON-IN-RIBBLESDALE	RIBBLEHEAD	16.6KM/ 10.3 MILES	635m	PEN-Y-GHENT	77–79	76–79
ANTICLOCKWISE: SECTION 2	RIBBLEHEAD	CHAPEL-LE-DALE	11.2KM/ 7 MILES	500M	WHERNSIDE	81	80
ANTICLOCKWISE: SECTION 3	CHAPEL-LE-DALE	HORTON-IN-RIBBLESDALE	11.6KM/ 7.2 MILES	465M	INGLE-BOROUGH	82–83	84
CLOCKWISE: SECTION 1	HORTON-IN-RIBBLESDALE	CHAPEL-LE-DALE	11.6KM/ 7.2 MILES	520M	INGLE-BOROUGH	82–83	86–87
CLOCKWISE: SECTION 2	CHAPEL-LE-DALE	RIBBLEHEAD	11.2KM/ 7 MILES	500M	WHERNSIDE	81	88–89
CLOCKWISE: SECTION 3	RIBBLEHEAD	HORTON-IN-RIBBLESDALE	16.6KM/ 10.3 MILES	580M	PEN-Y-GHENT	77–79	90–91

39.4km / 24.5 miles

13–14 / THE THREE PEAKS

The classic loop around the hills of Pen-y-ghent, Whernside and Ingleborough.

/ ESSENTIAL INFO
GRADE ● ● ● ●
DISTANCE **39.4KM/24.5 MILES**
ASCENT **1,600M**
TIME **10–15 HRS (WALKER)/ 5–8 HRS (RUNNER)**
START/FINISH **HORTON-IN-RIBBLESDALE, RIBBLEHEAD OR CHAPEL-LE-DALE**
START GRID REF **SD 807 725 (HORTON-IN-RIBBLESDALE); SD 765 792 (RIBBLEHEAD); SD 744 777 (CHAPEL-LE-DALE)**
START GPS **54.1488, -2.2959 (HORTON-IN-RIBBLESDALE); 54.2089, -2.3611 (RIBBLEHEAD); 54.1946, -2.3932 (CHAPEL-LE-DALE)**
OS MAP **OL2 YORKSHIRE DALES: SOUTHERN & WESTERN AREAS (1:25,000)**

/ OVERVIEW
A long and strenuous walk, with much ascent and therefore descent too, but an absolute classic with wide-ranging and ever-changing views. It's a full-on day out so be prepared, but there are also plenty of escape points should it all become too much. An adventure not to be forgotten. Plan ahead and you will have a great day.

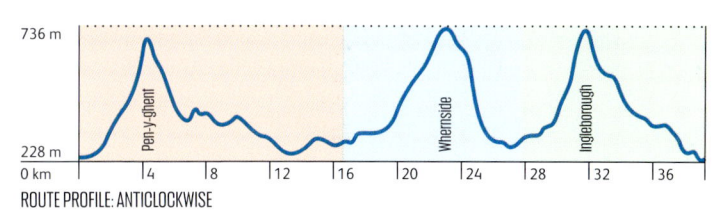

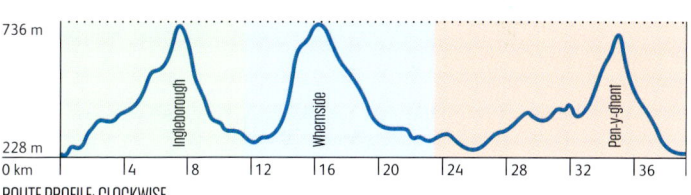

ROUTE PROFILE: ANTICLOCKWISE

ROUTE PROFILE: CLOCKWISE

13 / SECTION 1 (ANTICLOCKWISE): HORTON-IN-RIBBLESDALE TO RIBBLEHEAD

DISTANCE **16.6KM/10.3 MILES**
ASCENT **635M**

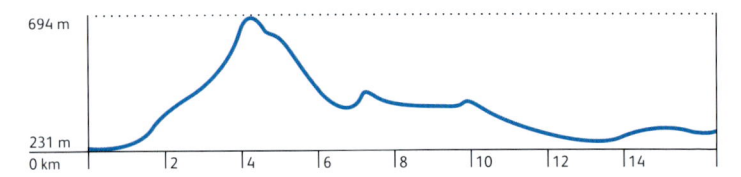

S It's likely that even if you aren't parked there, you will be using the toilets at the YDNP car park. **Turn right** out of the car park and head through the village to the church, following the road as it bends round past the church to the left. Cross the bridge and **turn left** up the lane: this is the **second** road junction on the left – make sure you have crossed the river. Follow the lane as it climbs and starts to curve right back round on itself. Just before the farm buildings take the footpath on the **left** – the gate here may be open or closed; just leave it as you found it. Then use the **middle gate of the three ahead of you** to enter the more open fellside. The farmer has clearly marked which is the correct gate to use – it's the one that's a national park footpath gate rather than a farm gate.

2 The path then climbs, sometimes steeply, generally parallel to the wall for 2km, passing through a couple of gates along the way. At the third gate you will meet the Pennine Way. **Turn left** and continue climbing towards Pen-y-ghent. The path here is generally paved and stepped but there are a few places where you will walk on the bedrock. The first rock step is the easier; on the second step you will probably end up using your hands as well. A flagged path then takes you up the final rise to the summit. First hill done.

3 Use the stiles to cross the summit wall and follow the signed route **north** down the Pennine Way/Three Peaks. This path starts off a bit loose but then becomes paved steps before becoming rough again. It is very clear to follow. There is a sharp bend to the **left** which is signposted just as you reach the impressive limestone cliffs. Continue down, now heading **west**, and on the main path to the crossroads at SD 822 742.

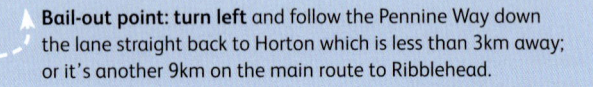

> **Bail-out point: turn left** and follow the Pennine Way down the lane straight back to Horton which is less than 3km away; or it's another 9km on the main route to Ribblehead.

13 / THE THREE PEAKS: ANTICLOCKWISE

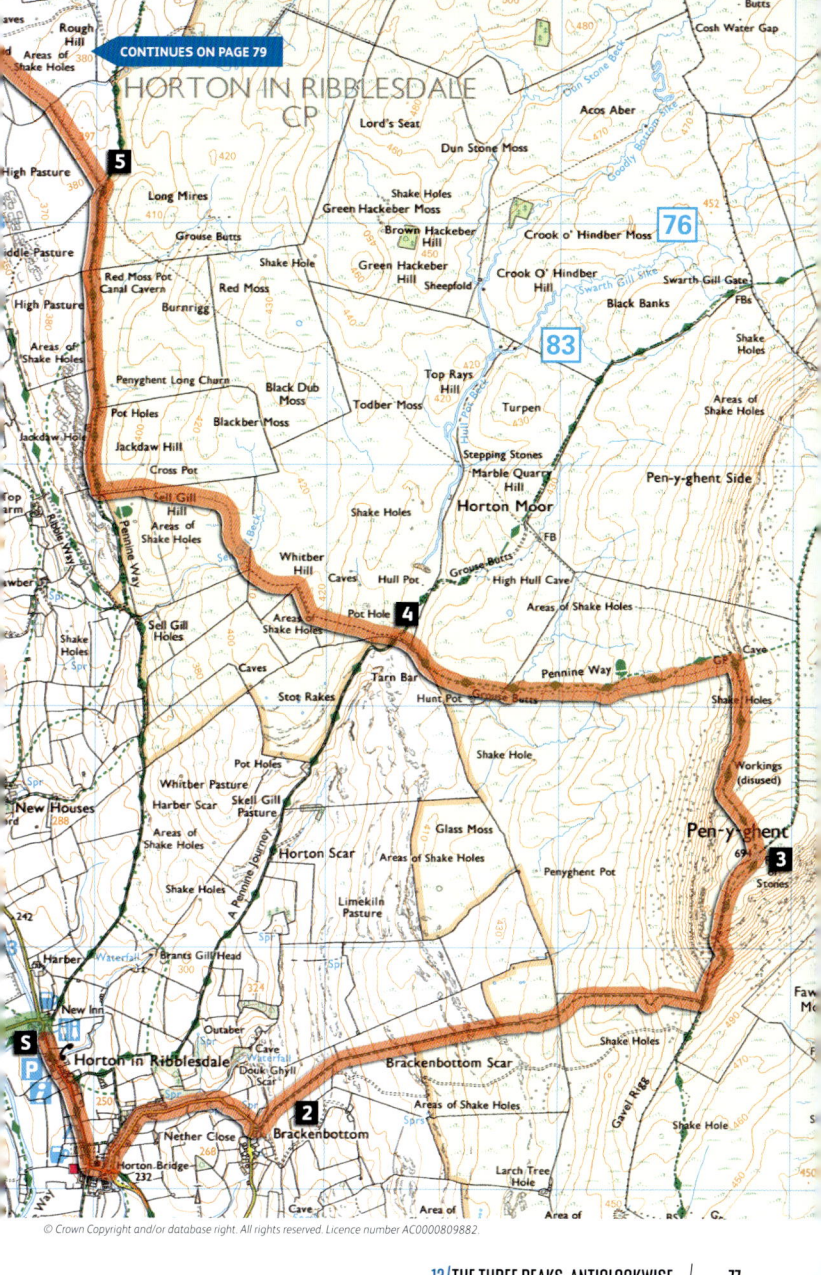

4 Continue **straight ahead**, climbing up a drumlin on a gravelled track. The made track is clear across the moor and drops down alongside a wall to join the Pennine Way again. **Turn right** and follow the track along a line of sinkholes, a sure sign you are back on to limestone terrain. Continue **straight ahead** through two gates and, where the way ahead starts to become more grassy, use the gate on the **left**.

5 Follow the gravelled path over yet another drumlin to a wall and gate. Continue **straight ahead** up a very short climb and then follow the broad grassy swathe **straight ahead** which then joins into a gravelled farm track. Follow this track as it goes through a gate, swings right and then joins the Pennine Bridleway. **Turn left** downhill and **turn right** along the next track. After a wall and a gate the farm track swings away right uphill; our path continues **straight ahead** across some rougher ground before rejoining the farm track down to a gate.

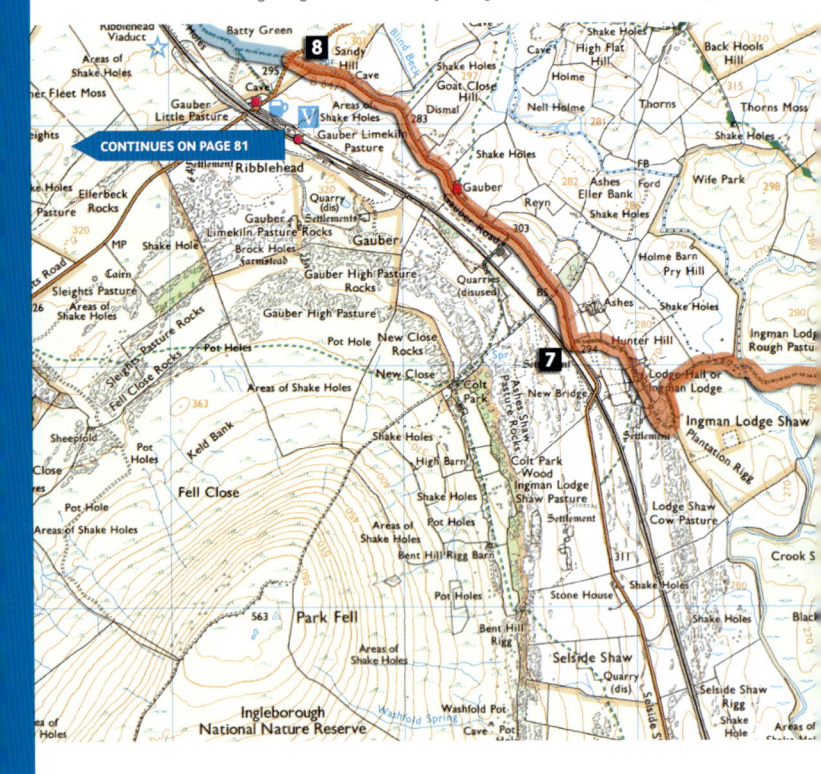

6 This is God's Bridge, a natural bridge formed by a short cave – this can be seen by peering down the riverbed to the right. It's also a good point to pick up some water. Continue down the farm track to a footbridge over Ling Gill Beck on the right-hand side of the farm buildings at Nether Lodge. Once through the gate **turn immediately left** and then pick up the big farm road as it comes out of the yard heading right. Follow this as it crosses rough pasture with a bridge over the young River Ribble. After the river the track starts to climb gently and curves round to the farm at Lodge Hall. Here you join tarmac. Keep **straight ahead** uphill to a gate and cattle grid just before the main road.

7 **Turn right** and follow the road to Ribblehead. There is a bit of a path on the verge at times, at other times not. The road can get very busy, so be aware.

At Ribblehead there is parking, often a tea van, the Station Inn and the railway station. The Station Inn has kindly provided Portaloos which can be used by walkers in their car park. They ask that you contribute to the running costs by making a donation or buying something in the pub. There are also toilets inside the pub for customers. Food is served 12–9 p.m. at the time of writing.

> **Bail-out point:** you can easily be picked up here or catch a train back to Horton or Settle.

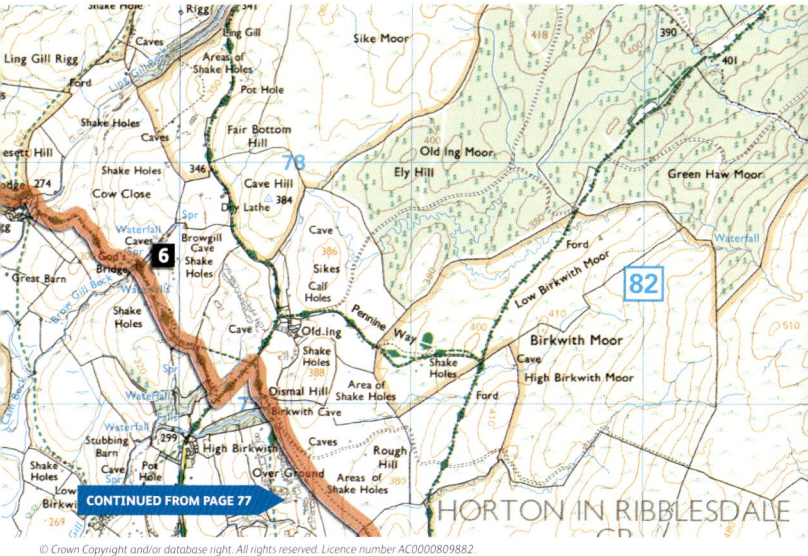

© Crown Copyright and/or database right. All rights reserved. Licence number AC0000809882.

13/THE THREE PEAKS: ANTICLOCKWISE

13 / SECTION 2 (ANTICLOCKWISE): RIBBLEHEAD TO CHAPEL-LE-DALE

DISTANCE **11.2KM/7 MILES**
ASCENT **500M**

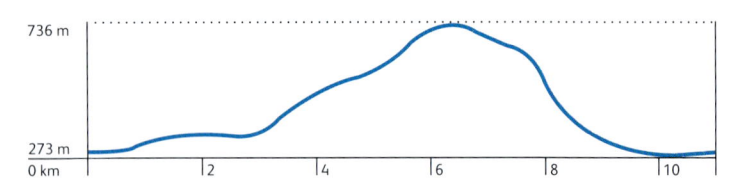

8 From the road junction take the gravelled path heading towards the viaduct. Join a larger track but keep **straight on** running parallel with the railway and up the steps. Continue **straight ahead** on this clear track.

9 About 600m after Blea Moor signal box there is a fork in the path (SD 760 812) – **fork left** and drop down to cross the river. The path then climbs slightly to cross the railway, steepens up Slack Hill and then gets gentler again.

10 The path up Whernside leads clearly off on the **left**. It's the obvious path – signposted over the stile. Follow this path up and around to the top of Whernside where there is a shelter; the trig point is through the drystone wall. Second hill done.

11 From the summit, continue **straight ahead** on the broad path down the ridge and then **bear left** down the steep descent which has now been paved and stepped. As you pass through a gate the gradient becomes gentler.

12 At the next gate **turn right** and then **immediately left** on to the gravel road. It becomes tarmacked very quickly. Follow this all the way to the main road and **turn left**. Pass the Old Hill Inn and then look for a gate on the **right** just before a stone built small building.

Not far before you join the main road is Philpin Farm campsite which caters for tents but also has toilets, water and snacks available, with a snack bar at weekends during summer. See page 85. Please note the car parking here is for campers and not for support vehicles which must stay on the main road.

> **Bail-out option:** it is straightforward to be picked up from Philpin Lane or the Old Hill Inn. Philpin Farm has a landline that can be borrowed in case of emergencies if you have no phone signal.

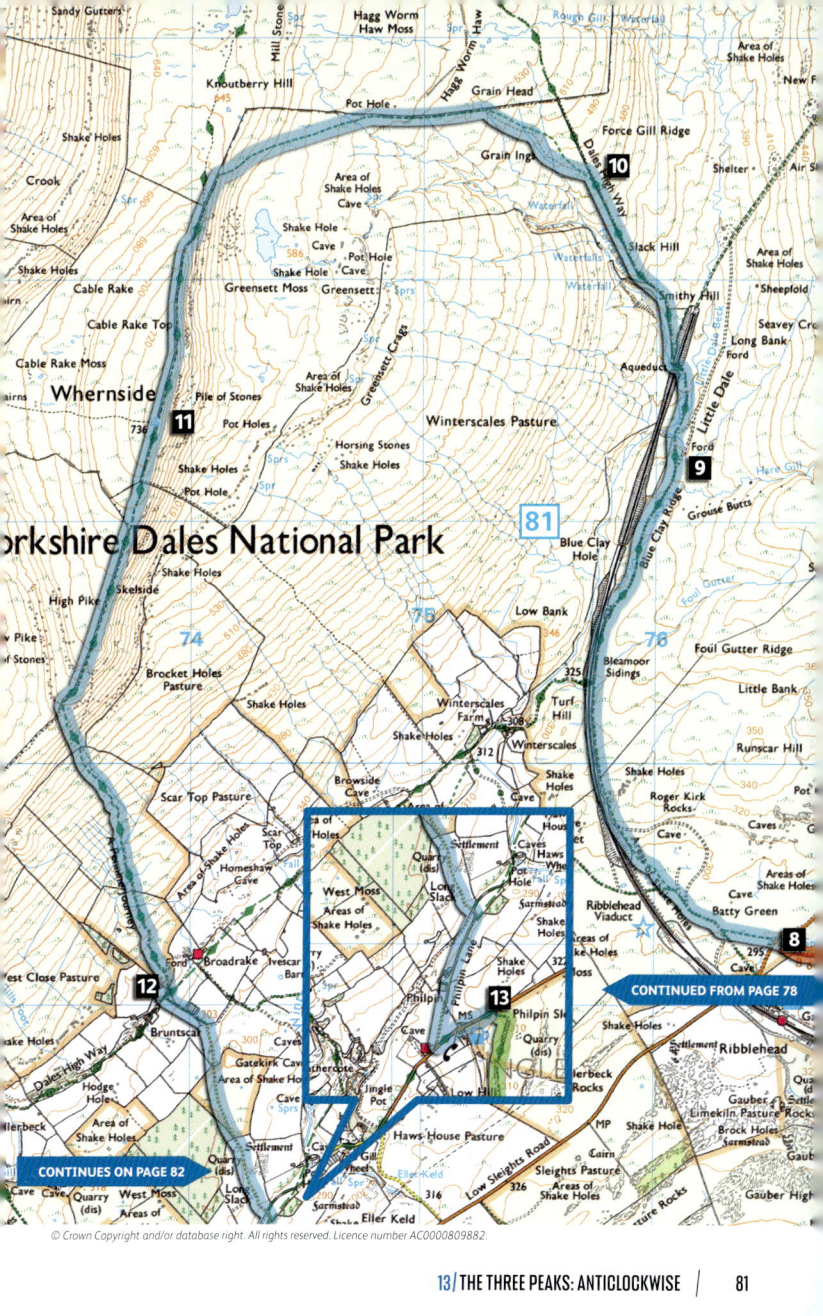

13 / THE THREE PEAKS: ANTICLOCKWISE   81

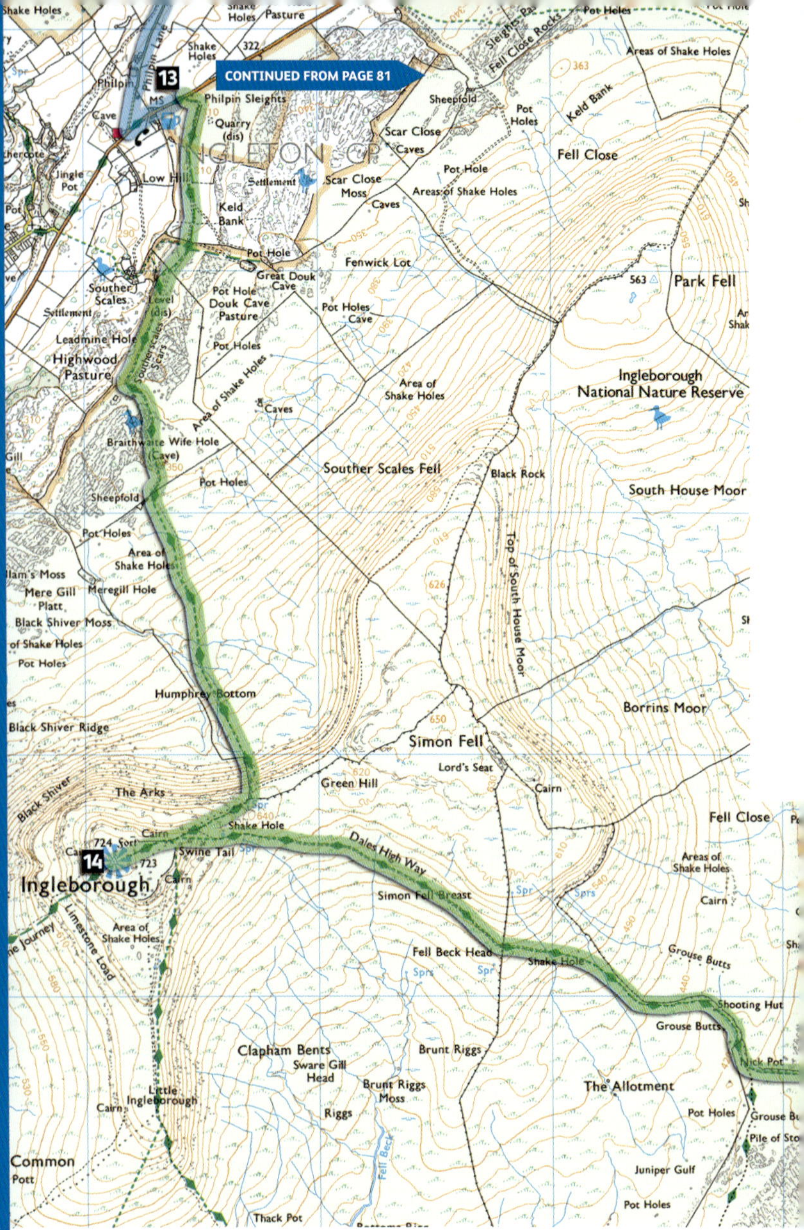
CONTINUED FROM PAGE 81
13
14
Philpin Sleights
Shake Holes
Pasture
Philpin
Quarry (dis)
Cave
Jingle Pot
Low Hill
Settlement
Scar Close Moss
Scar Close Caves
Sheepfold
Pot Holes
Keld Bank
Fell Close
Pot Hole
Areas of Shake Holes
Caves
Sleights Pasture
Fell Close Rocks
Pot Holes
Areas of Shake Holes
363
Fenwick Lot
Great Douk Cave
Souther Scales
Settlement
Douk Cave Pasture
Level (dis)
Pot Holes Cave
563
Park Fell
Leadmine Hole
Highwood Pasture
Southerscales Scars
Area of Shake Holes
Caves
Area of Shake Holes
Ingleborough National Nature Reserve
Braithwaite Wife Hole (Cave)
Southern Scales Fell
Black Rock
South House Moor
Sheepfold
Pot Holes
Area of Shake Holes
626
Top of South House Moor
Mere Gill Platt
Meregill Hole
Black Shiver Moss
Pot Holes
Humphrey Bottom
Borrins Moor
Black Shiver Ridge
650
Simon Fell
Lord's Seat
Green Hill
Cairn
The Arks
Black Shiver
Shake Hole
Fell Close
724
723
Swine Tail
Ingleborough
Dales High Way
Areas of Shake Holes
Simon Fell Breast
Cairn
Limestone Load
Area of Shake Holes
Fell Beck Head
Shake Hole
Grouse Butts
Shooting Hut
Grouse Butts
Clapham Bents
Sware Gill Head
Brunt Riggs
Brunt Riggs Moss
The Allotment
Little Ingleborough
Cairn
Riggs
Pot Holes
Common
Pott
Fell Beck
Juniper Gulf
Pot Holes
Thack Pot

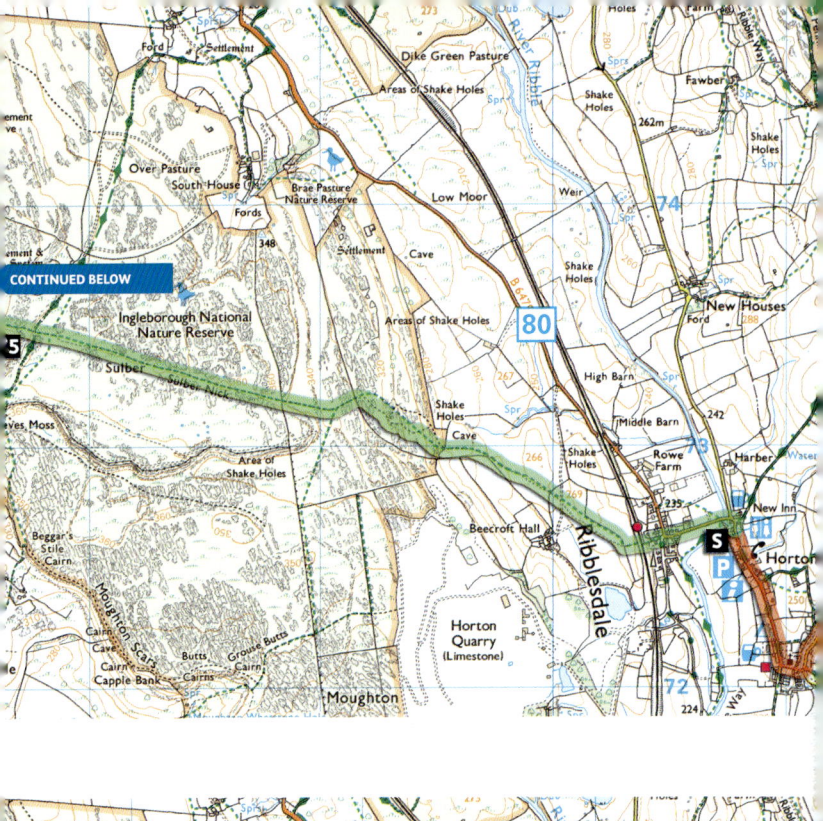

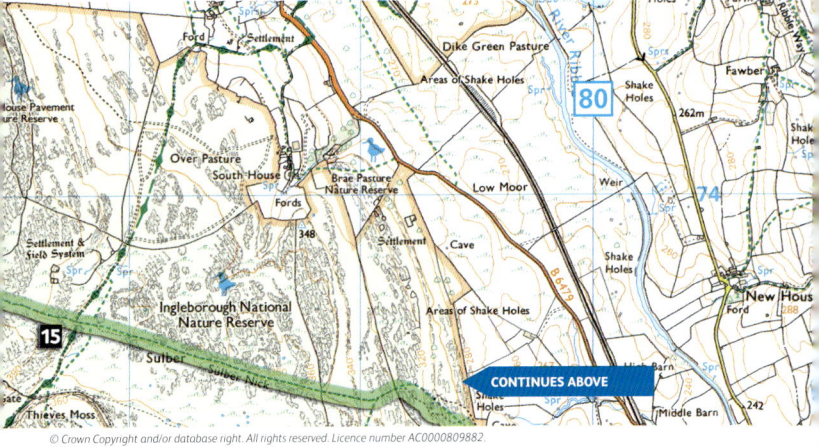

13 / THE THREE PEAKS: ANTICLOCKWISE

13 / SECTION 3 (ANTICLOCKWISE): CHAPEL-LE-DALE TO HORTON-IN-RIBBLESDALE

DISTANCE 11.6KM/7.2 MILES
ASCENT 465M

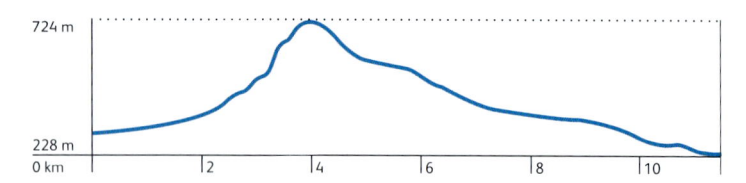

13 From the gate follow the wide track past the splendid lime kiln and **straight ahead** through several fields of improved pastureland. Continue to follow this track as it swings left and starts to ascend more steeply. You will pass Braithwaite Wife Hole on the left and pass through another wall. Continue **straight ahead** on the clear path which eventually climbs very steeply up the flank of Ingleborough and then heads **right**. Just before you reach the final rocky steps keep an eye out for a path coming in from the left – this is your return path to Horton. Climb up through the rocky section and make your way over the summit plateau to the trig point. Third and final hill done.

14 Return the way you came to the rocky steps. In low cloud or mist it is all too easy to make a mistake at this point, especially if this is your last hill and you are tired. You need to head **north-east** to find the rocky steps again. Go back down the rocky section but **head right** at the path junction, sometimes but not always signed. The path descends fairly steeply and then starts to level out – if you start heading very steeply down you are on the wrong path, north back to Chapel. Check you are heading eastwards. Continue down the obvious path across the side of Simon Fell. Just after an old shooting hut and the second gate there is a split in the path. **Keep left** to stay on the Horton path which runs parallel to the wall at first and then continues **straight ahead**.

15 Keep **straight ahead** at the junction with the Pennine Bridleway (SD 777 734). The path remains mostly clear and obvious, plus there are some cairns to mark out the less clear section. You drop back on to pastureland, and while the path is clear enough, this can be one of the soggiest parts of the walk after rain. It can also be slippery – steady away on wet grass, one of the worst surfaces to walk on. The path comes out at the railway crossing. There are plans to build a footbridge here – it will be clearly signposted. Head **straight ahead** down the hill to the main road. Follow this up to the village and round over the two bridges back to the car park.

MOUNTAIN WALKS **YORKSHIRE THREE PEAKS**

GOOD TO KNOW

PUBLIC TRANSPORT AND ACCESS

Both Horton and Ribblehead are on the Settle–Carlisle Railway, with trains to Settle, Leeds and Carlisle. DalesBus service 11 runs between Settle and Horton.

There is a national park car park with toilets in Horton, plus extra parking at the northern end of the village in a field. There is parking at Ribblehead around the road junction, and a little parking on the road round Chapel-le-Dale. All parking gets very busy at weekends and during the summer. Arrive early – though you will anyway if you're taking on the route in a single day.

WHEN TO WALK IT

In terms of terrain underfoot, the whole walk is pretty weatherproof due to the maintained paths. What you really need is enough light and an early enough start. May to September has the light and hopefully the weather. What is a blustery breeze in the valley will make walking on the tops difficult, and very tiring. On hot sunny days be aware there is very little shelter anywhere on the walk. It's also wise to avoid race days: the Three Peaks cyclo-cross race is usually the last weekend in September, and the fell race the end of April.

TERRAIN AND NAVIGATION

There is a lot of ascent and descent, sometimes on steep paths and sometimes on bedrock which can be slippery. Generally, the paths are well-maintained and the bogs of the previous century covered with flagged and made paths. Route finding is straightforward, well signposted and easy to follow, with the only real navigational challenge being on the top of Ingleborough where it is crucial to get the right path off the summit at a point in the walk when you are likely to be very tired. In mist and low cloud this may require a map and compass – and the ability to use both.

FACILITIES AND REFRESHMENTS

Horton: toilets in the national park car park, pubs in the village, occasionally a shop with snacks but at the time of writing no cafe.

Ribblehead: the Station Inn does food all day and has toilets in the pub for customers, plus Portaloos in the car park for walkers. A water tap is also available. Please contribute if you use these facilities.

Chapel-le-Dale: Philpin Farm campsite right on the route not long before you get to the main road has toilets, water, coffee and snack machines, plus a barn offering shelter. There is a snack bar at weekends during the summer. Again, pay for what you use. The Old Hill Inn is occasionally open but don't rely on it.

Water is available around the walk if you take a water filter. It also means you are carrying less weight at any one point and can drink without fear of running out, especially on hot days.

DOGS AND KIDS

It's a very long way, it's a very tough walk. Think carefully about whether your dog or child is going to be happy and comfortable.

POINTS OF INTEREST

It's a long walk through fascinating terrain, carved by ice and water, with man's influence added on top. There are three hills of rugged distinction, each with their own character and feel. On a clear day the views are spectacular and include the other two peaks and the wider reaches of the Dales national park, plus the Howgills, the Lakes and Morecambe Bay.

14 / SECTION 1 (CLOCKWISE): HORTON-IN-RIBBLESDALE TO CHAPEL-LE-DALE

DISTANCE 11.6KM/7.2 MILES   **MAP PAGES 82–83**
ASCENT 520M

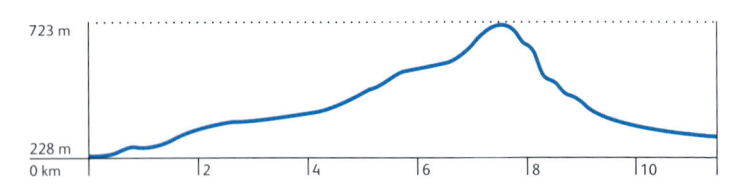

S After using the toilets in the YDNP car park, **turn left** and follow the road through the village over the bridges and head towards the station. The main Ribblehead road swings right at a crossroads – keep **straight ahead** here into the station itself, using the right-hand side of the driveway, and cross the railway on the crossing to pick up the path on the other side. There are plans to install a footbridge here, not only for the right of way but to allow passengers to cross to the other platform more safely. Whatever final form the bridge takes, it will be clearly marked. After a gate the path enters fields but is an easy line to follow. After rain, this is likely to be one of the soggiest sections of the whole walk. It can also be quite slippery. Thankfully, you soon come off the pastureland and on to a firmer, limestone track. Keep **straight ahead** on this track through Sulber Nick.

15 Continue **straight ahead** at the junction with the Pennine Bridleway (SD 777 734) and continue to follow the path as it steadily but relentlessly climbs under Simon Fell. As you near the top of Ingleborough, the path steepens, and then joins another coming in from the right – this is your onward journey once you have visited the summit. A section through rocky steps, man-placed and natural, brings you to the summit plateau and across to the trig point. First hill done.

14 Retrace your path to the rocky steps. In low cloud or mist it is all too easy to make a mistake at this point. The path to Chapel and the one you came up are in the north-east corner of the plateau: if you don't go back down the rocky steps you just came up, you're going the wrong way. At the path split you saw previously **keep left/straight ahead**, continuing **north-east**. After a wall the path descends very steeply – you should be heading in a **northerly** direction at this point. Thankfully the path gets less steep and becomes a mix of flags and a bit of boarding across the worst of the soggy moor. After a wall when you return to limestone, the gradient is far more gentle and the path a mix of limestone and grass. Follow it past the huge sink hole of Braithwaite Wife Hole and through Southerscales Scars. Continue and emerge through a gate on to the main road.

Ingleborough from Ribblehead. © John Coefield

Just left down the road is the Old Hill Inn which may or may not be open – it's best not to rely on it. Otherwise, refreshments and toilets are available at Philpin Farm campsite not far along the lane. There's a snack bar at weekends during summer, and vending machines supplying coffee and calories at other times. As ever, pay for what you use and support the good people offering such handy services. Please note the car parking here is for campers and not for support vehicles which need to stay on the main road.

> **Bail-out option:** it is straightforward to be picked up from Philpin Lane or the Old Hill Inn. Philpin Farm has a landline that can be borrowed in case of emergencies if you have no phone signal.

14/ THE THREE PEAKS: CLOCKWISE

Hart's tongue fern in a limestone gryke. © Hannah Collingridge

14 / SECTION 2 (CLOCKWISE): CHAPEL-LE-DALE TO RIBBLEHEAD

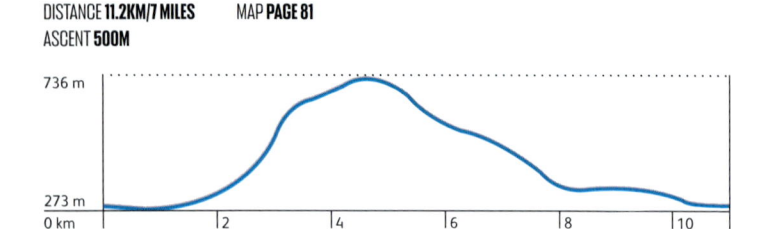

DISTANCE **11.2KM/7 MILES** MAP **PAGE 81**
ASCENT **500M**

13 From the gate, **turn left** down the road and then **right** at the next road junction on to Philpin Lane – there's a gate and a cattle grid together, and it's signposted to the campsite and the bunk barn. Follow this road until the end of the tarmac and take the **left fork** effectively straight ahead on the track. **Turn right** at the T-junction of tracks and then **turn left** to start climbing.

12 Keep climbing on the obvious path which has steps to help with erosion before emerging on to the ridge. Keep on the path, bearing **right**, and follow it to the summit of Whernside. There is a shelter at the top and the trig point is through the drystone wall. Second hill done.

88 / MOUNTAIN WALKS **YORKSHIRE THREE PEAKS**

Mountain thyme. © Hannah Collingridge

11 Come back through the wall and **head left**, initially **north**, down the ridge following the path down and round the fellside.

10 At a stile you join the old road to Dent (SD 757 824) – **turn right** and continue downhill. After Slack Hill you cross the railway and the gradient becomes more gentle.

9 The path is clear and obvious as you run roughly parallel with the railway towards the road at Ribblehead. There's a set of steps which drop you down to the level of Ribblehead viaduct floor where you join a larger track. If you want the facilities of the Station Inn or the railway station, keep straight on. Otherwise, look for a path heading **left** at around SD 762 793 which leads directly to the road junction. If you miss it, you can pick up the main road at the end of the larger track and drop back down to the junction.

At Ribblehead there is parking, often a tea van, the Station Inn and the railway station. The Station Inn has kindly provided Portaloos in their car park which can be used by walkers. They ask that you contribute to the running costs by making a donation or buying something in the pub. There are also toilets inside the pub for customers. Food is served 12–9 p.m. at the time of writing.

> **Bail-out point:** you can easily be picked up here or can catch a train back to Horton or Settle.

14 / SECTION 3 (CLOCKWISE): RIBBLEHEAD TO HORTON-IN-RIBBLESDALE

DISTANCE **16.6KM/10.3 MILES**   MAP **PAGE 77–79**
ASCENT **580M**

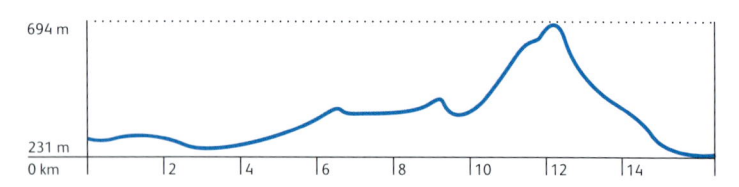

8 From the T-junction at Ribblehead, head **south-east** down the B6479 Horton and Settle road for about 2km. Be aware that this road can get busy; there is a bit of a path on the left-hand side of the road in several places but that will likely have walkers coming the other way and doesn't allow you to face oncoming traffic. Shortly after passing the driveway to Ashes Farm B & B on the left, **turn left** down a tarmacked lane – there's a gate and a cattlegrid. It should also be signposted but it can be easy to miss.

7 Head down the lane and follow it through the farmyard. Continue **straight ahead** and keep following the track as it bends round and heads over the River Ribble and up to Nether Lodge farm. Pick up the path to the **left** in front of the farm buildings, then go **right** through a gate in the corner of the wall heading over the footbridge to join a track. Follow this up to a gate with a stream coming in from the left.

6 This is God's Bridge, a natural limestone bridge – the stream runs in a cave underneath. Go through the gate and continue **straight ahead**. The farm track heads off to the left, but keep **straight ahead** along a grassier path which then rejoins the farm track. Continue through another gate until you reach the Pennine Bridleway. **Turn left**, uphill, and then **right** at the next junction. Follow this track, through a gate, and then continue **straight ahead** on the grassy swathe through the pastureland. After a wall you go up and over a drumlin and down to the Pennine Way.

5 **Turn right** along the Pennine Way, continuing along the track for just over 1km until you see a signposted path on the left heading up by a wall (SD 810 748). Take this and follow the gravelled path as it winds up and round several drumlins down to the crossroads at Tarn Bar (SD 823 742).

View south to Pen-y-ghent and the Pennine Way. © Hannah Collingridge

> **Bail-out point: turn right** and follow the Pennine Way down the lane straight back to Horton, which is less than 3km away and downhill. This will miss out the ascent of Pen-y-ghent.

4 Keep **straight ahead** at the crossroads and head upwards on the clear track. There's a **sharp right** turn under the limestone cliffs, signed, and then the path climbs, sometimes rough underfoot, sometimes paved, all the way to the top of Pen-y-ghent. Third and final hill done.

3 If you do not fancy the scramble down the nose of Pen-y-ghent which can be tricky if you don't like exposure or the wind is gusting, then return to Tarn Bar and take the Pennine Way down to the village (as per the bail-out option above). Otherwise, cross the wall and follow the flagged path **right** down to the rock steps. The higher step is trickier and you will need to use your hands. After the second step the path descends to a junction. The Pennine Way continues ahead, but take the gate on the **right** to start descending, roughly parallel with the wall, to Brackenbottom Farm.

2 One gate takes you into the farmyard – head **straight ahead** to another gate and **turn right** down the road. Follow this to the main village road, **turn right** and continue through the village, past the church, back to the car park.

14/THE THREE PEAKS: CLOCKWISE

/ THREE-DAY ITINERARIES

So, you fancy walking the famous route but realise it's maybe too much for one day or you don't want to be walking against the clock? Slowing the whole thing down means you have time to properly explore points of interest along the way, instead of being head down and rushing. There are various options for splitting the route across three days.

- Find a **willing friend** who is able to drop you off and pick you up at the start and finish of each section, returning you to your accommodation each night. This has the advantage of being very flexible, and you will not need to carry too much stuff each day. It does however rely on having a friend who is willing to sacrifice three days of their life so you can go for a walk. Perhaps you'll need to return the favour one day?
- **Camp.** There are campsites suitable for tents at Horton and Chapel so it makes sense to start a camping Three Peaks at Ribblehead as this is the area without a campsite. Sadly, it's not technically legal to wild camp without the landowner's prior permission in England and Wales.
- The luxury of a **real bed** in between the sections. You'll have to book your accommodation well in advance, but it's possible to have a prepared bed and meal on your way round.
  - Horton has the biggest selection of accommodation, ranging from tent camping, bunkhouse, glamping, B & Bs, guesthouses and pubs.
  - At or close to Ribblehead there is the Station Inn which has rooms and a bunkhouse, plus there is Gauber Bunk Barn and Ashes Farm, both on the road section just south of Ribblehead.
  - Chapel-le-Dale has the Old Hill Inn and Broadrake Bunkbarn, so by no means as much choice.
  - When planning, bear in mind seasonal operations and restrictions such as bunkbarns being restricted for sole use at weekends, and some places requiring a two-night stay.
- **Use the train.** Staying either at Ribblehead or Horton, you can use the Settle–Carlisle railway to join up your trip. You'll need to use the Whernside from Ribblehead walk earlier in the book (page 59) to make a circular back to the station. For Ingleborough, you'll need to make a link between Philpin Lane and Ribblehead via Ivescar and Gunnerfleet Farm.
- Walk with a friend who also has **a car** and do a complicated dropping off of one car at the end of the section before returning to the start to walk that section. Or walk from opposite ends, swapping keys mid route. Lots of potential for mishap, and it really doesn't help the car parking situation in the national park!

/ TWO-DAY ITINERARIES

Walking the route over two days gives a good length walk on both days, but still allows plenty of time to enjoy the route. If you start from Horton, then Ribblehead is about halfway round. Starting from Chapel doesn't really split into two sections very evenly. Your options are similar to those for a three-day walk but with the following observations:

- **A camping trip** would be best started at Ribblehead with the overnight at Horton – this gives you the option of walking clockwise or anticlockwise.
- **Real beds:** more are available in Horton than at Ribblehead, but you'll still need to book ahead and be prepared.
- **Train:** you can use the Settle–Carlisle line between Horton and Ribblehead to get back to your starting point.

/ HOW ABOUT TWO HILLS IN A DAY?

It's possible to use the main Three Peaks route and a little bit of creativity to join two hills together for a longer day trip. Here are some ideas to get your imagination flowing.

- From Horton, follow the route up Pen-y-ghent and then Whernside but make your way back to Ribblehead and use the train to return to Horton.
- From Horton, head up Ingleborough but then walk over Simon Fell and Park Fell, dropping down to Gauber Road; turn right and pick up the Three Peaks route to return via Pen-y-ghent.
- From Ingleton, head up Ingleborough via Crina Bottom, head down to Chapel and up Whernside before retracing your steps as far as the descent but then use the ridge path and Oddies Lane to return.

/ EXPLORATION

If you are taking your time here are some suggestions for a bit of exploration.

- **Hunt Pot:** on the side of Pen-y-ghent at SD 826 740. Small grassy trods head off the path to the stream.
- **Hull Pot:** head up the bridleway from Tarn Bar to SD 824 745.
- **God's Bridge:** explore the cave under the bridge at SD 798 775.
- **Settle–Carlisle aqueduct:** have a closer look at the combined viaduct and aqueduct at SD 760 816.
- **Force Gill:** wander up to the waterfall SD 758 819.
- **Great Douk Cave:** signed off the route to Ingleborough at SD 747 770. The cave is hidden in a walled enclosure of trees.
- **Nick and Sulber pots:** access these using the stile at SD 772 736 where the Ingleborough path meets a cross wall. Follow the thin grassy trods to the pots.

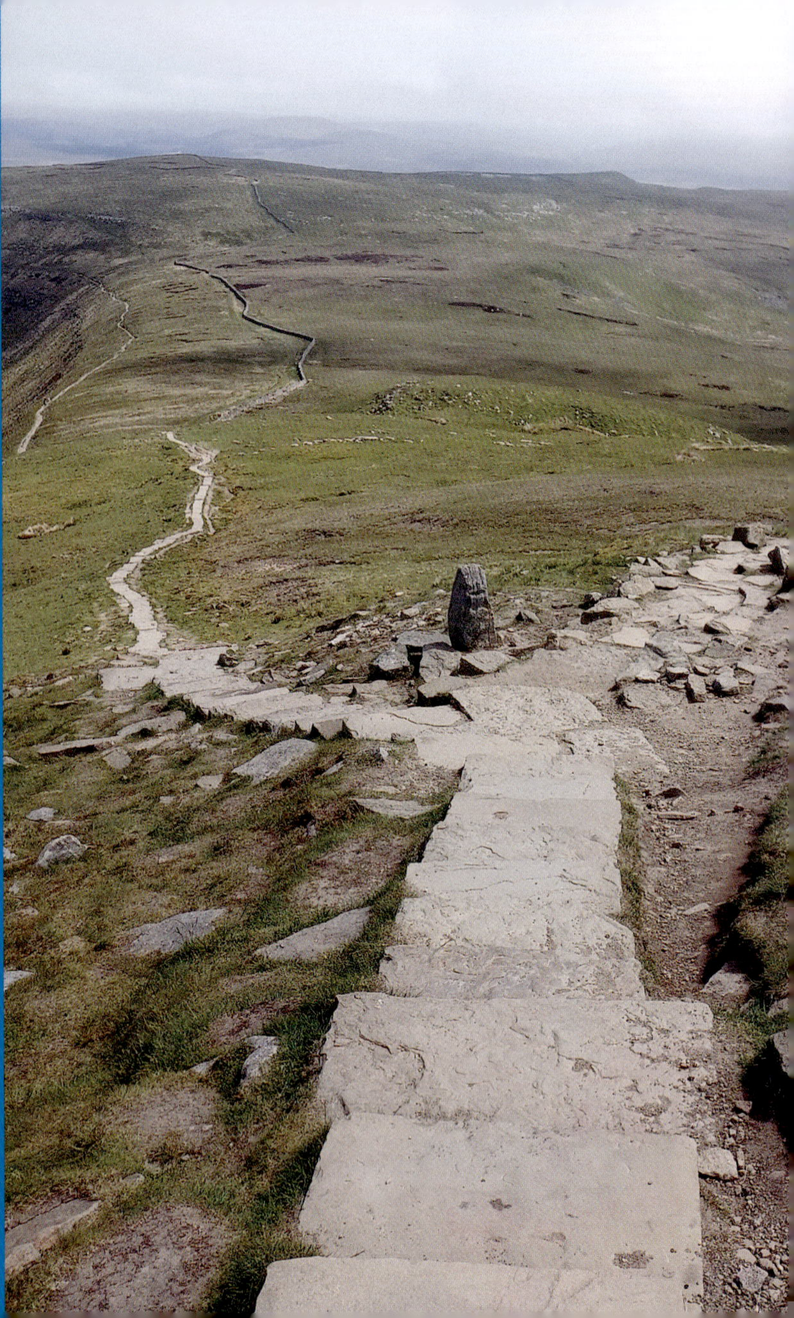

47km / 29.2 miles

15 / SUPER THREE PEAKS

Something a little different from the normal Three Peaks route – the 'Super Three Peaks', starting and finishing in Ingleton.

/ ESSENTIAL INFO
GRADE ● ● ● ●
DISTANCE **47KM/29.2 MILES**
ASCENT **1,785M**
TIME **11–16 HRS (WALKER)/6–10 HRS (RUNNER)**
START/FINISH **MAIN CAR PARK IN INGLETON**
START GRID REF **SD 695 729**
START GPS **54.1519, -2.4682**
OS MAP **OL2 YORKSHIRE DALES: SOUTHERN & WESTERN AREAS (1:25,000)**

/ OVERVIEW
Maybe you've done the Three Peaks, but so has everyone else. Here's an alternative route from Ingleton – the same Three Peaks, obviously, but with a different start and finish and fewer easy bail-out options. Bit longer, bit more ascent, bit tougher overall. The final descent down the ridge of Whernside is on far narrower paths than the rest, and it is not waymarked. As with our classic Three Peaks routes (pages 75–93), this route splits fairly well into three sections, between Ingleton and Horton, Horton and Ribblehead, and Ribblehead and Ingleton.

/ DIRECTIONS
As with our classic Three Peaks route, the directions for this extended Three Peaks from Ingleton are split into three sections: the first from Ingleton to Horton via Ingleborough; the second from Horton to Ribblehead via Pen-y-ghent; and the third from Ribblehead back to Ingleton via Whernside. Simply refer to the section you are on at the time.

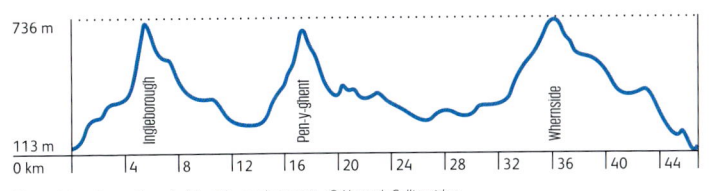

The path junction north-east of Ingleborough summit. © Hannah Collingridge

15 / SECTION 1: INGLETON TO HORTON-IN-RIBBLESDALE

DISTANCE **13.2KM/8.2 MILES**
ASCENT **630M**

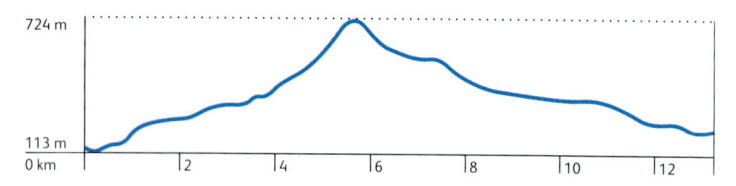

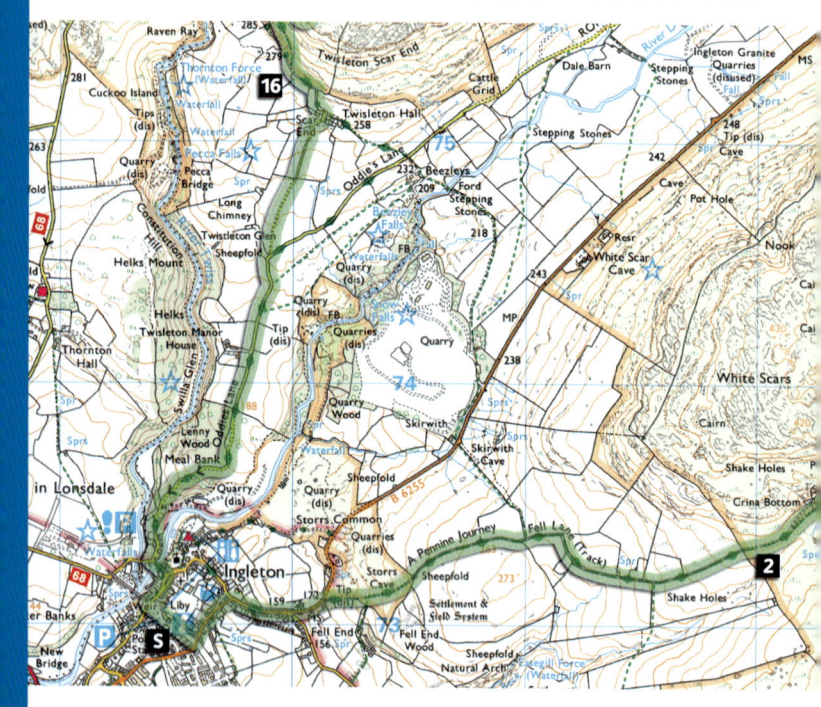

S With your back to the community centre in the main car park, **turn left** to the road and then **left** up the road towards Hawes. The roads bends round to the right, becoming shaded by trees, and the back road to Clapham is on the right. The pavement runs out and there is a short, walled section after which a track leads off to the **right: take this** – it should be signposted as a bridleway to *Ingleborough*. Follow the track which levels out a bit after the initial climb and becomes walled. Go through a gate at SD 719 733 and the track and vistas open out as you enter access land.

2 This is Crina Bottom and a splendid spot it is, too. Continue **straight ahead**, keep **right** at the fork, and follow the rougher track as it starts to climb. It steepens and gets rougher as you leave the limestone but much of the path has been built to help with erosion. There are three steep sections with tantalisingly flatter bits in between before you reach the summit of Ingleborough. The trig point is straight in front of you. The cairns which mark the final section of path can be handy in poor visibility. First hill done.

3 Head to the **north-east** corner of the summit plateau to find the path with natural rocky steps. After a short descent there is a path junction, sometimes signed, sometimes not: head **right**. The path descends fairly steeply and then starts to level out – if you start heading very steeply down you are on the path north to Chapel; check you are heading eastwards – if you are not, you are going the wrong way. Continue down the obvious path across the side of Simon Fell. Just after an old shooting hut and the second gate there is a split in the path.

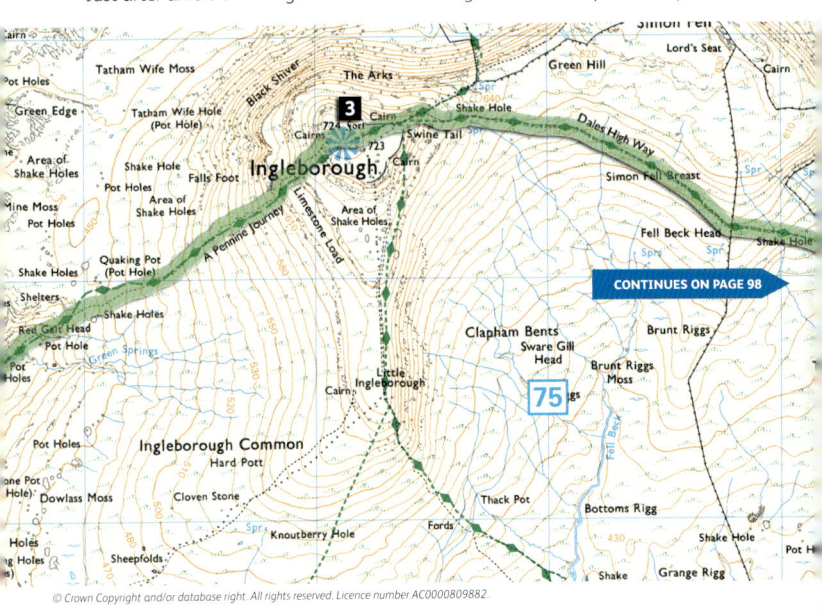

4 **Keep left** to stay on the Horton path which runs parallel to the wall at first and then continues **straight ahead**. Keep **straight ahead** at the junction with the Pennine Bridleway (SD 777 734). The path remains mostly clear and obvious, plus there are some cairns to mark out the less clear section. You drop back on to pastureland, and while the path is clear enough, this can be one of the soggiest parts of the walk after rain. It can also be slippery – steady away on wet grass, one of the worst surfaces to walk on. The path comes out at the railway crossing. There are plans to build a footbridge here – it will be clearly signposted. Head **straight ahead** down the hill to the main road. Follow this up to the village and round over the two bridges to the car park.

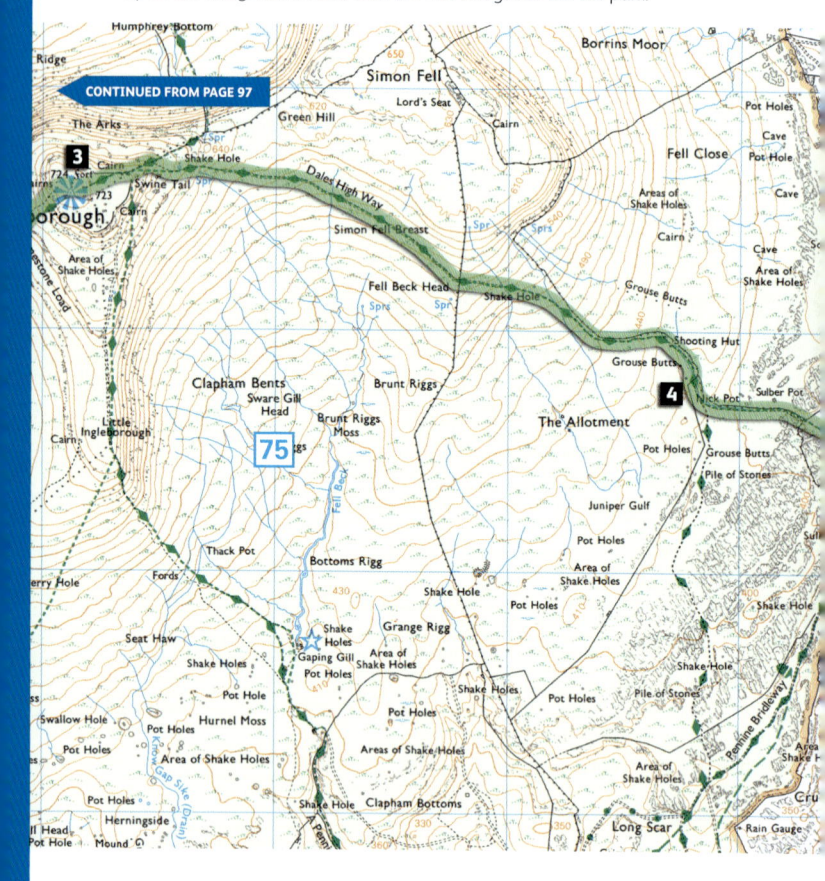

Horton has the only reasonable public transport options en route, with a railway station on the Settle–Carlisle line, and bus connections (DalesBus 11) to Settle. There are a couple of pubs in the village and a small shop which is sometimes open for limited refreshments. To get back to Ingleton will mean a train/bus to Settle and then another bus to Ingleton. Or an expensive taxi. Public toilets are available in the national park car park which is passed on the route.

15 / SECTION 2: HORTON-IN-RIBBLESDALE TO RIBBLEHEAD

DISTANCE **16.6KM/10.3 MILES**
ASCENT **635M**

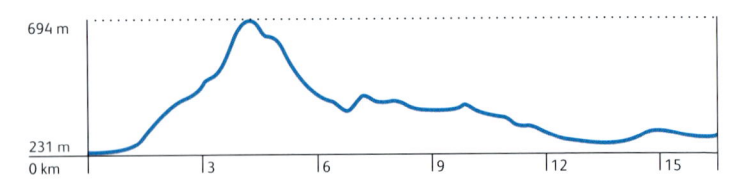

5 Continue **straight ahead** past the car park and head through the village to the church, following the road as it bends round past the church to the left. Cross the bridge and **turn left** up the lane. This is the **second** road junction on the left — make sure you have crossed the river. Follow the lane as it climbs and starts to curve back round on itself. Just before the farm buildings take the footpath on the **left** – the gate here may be open or closed; just leave it as you find it. Then use the **middle gate of the three ahead of you** on to the more open fellside. The farmer has clearly marked which is the correct gate to use — it's the one that's a national park footpath gate rather than a farm gate.

6 The path climbs, sometimes steeply, generally parallel to the wall for 2km, passing through a couple of gates along the way. At the third gate you meet the Pennine Way. **Turn left** and continue climbing. The path here is generally paved and stepped but there are a few places where you walk on the bedrock. The first rock step is the easiest; on the second step you will probably end up using your hands as well. A flagged path then takes you up the final rise to the summit of Pen-y-ghent. Second hill done.

7 Use the stiles to cross the summit wall and follow the signed route **north** down the Pennine Way/Three Peaks. This path starts off a bit loose but then becomes paved steps before becoming rougher again. It is very clear to follow. There is a sharp bend to the **left** which is signposted just as you reach the impressive limestone cliffs. Continue down, now heading **west**, and on the main path to the crossroads at SD 822 742.

8 Continue **straight ahead**, climbing up a drumlin on a gravelled track. The made track is clear across the moor and drops down alongside a wall to rejoin the Pennine Way. **Turn right** and follow the track along a line of sinkholes, a sure sign you are back on to limestone. Continue **straight ahead** through two gates, and where the way ahead starts to become more grassy, use the gate on the **left**.

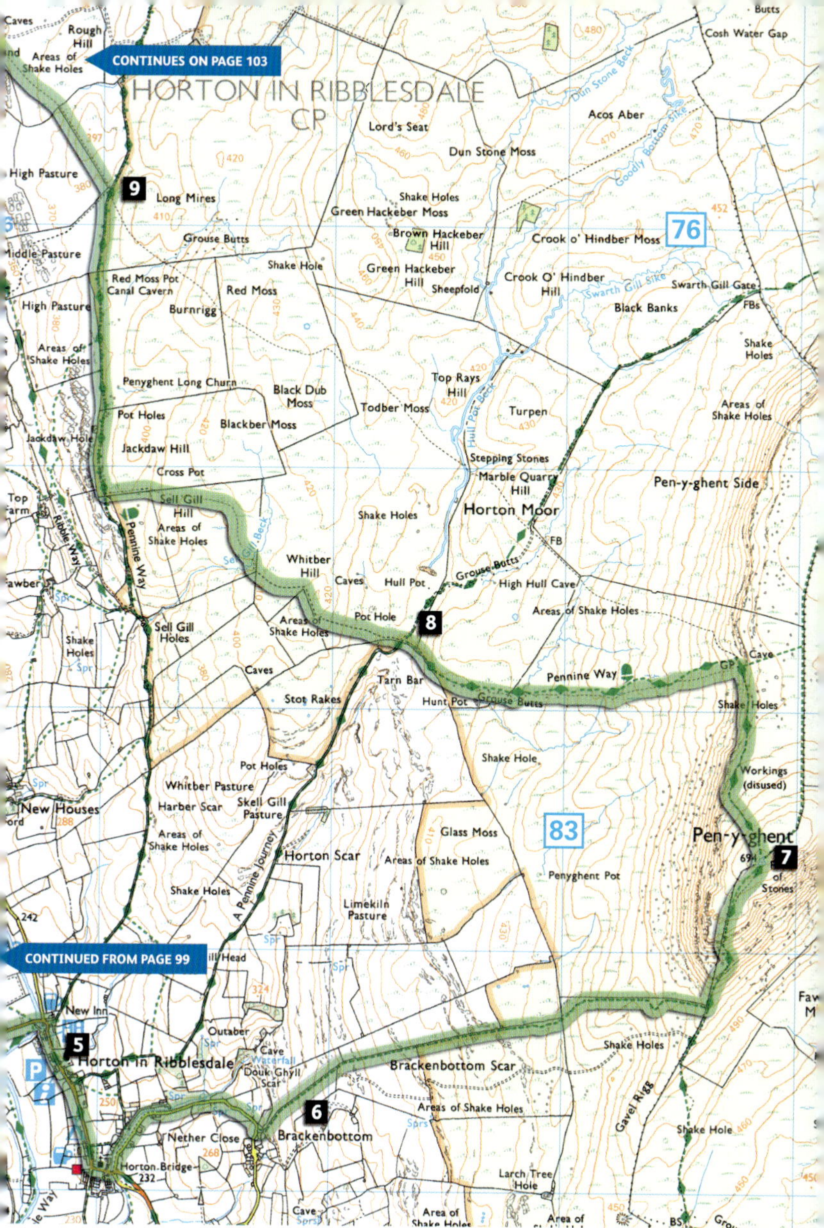

© Crown Copyright and/or database right. All rights reserved. Licence number AC0000809882.

9 Follow the gravelled path over yet another drumlin to a wall and gate. Continue **straight ahead** up a very short climb and then follow the broad grassy swathe **straight ahead** which then joins into a gravelled farm track. Follow this track as it goes through a gate, swings right and then joins the Pennine Bridleway. **Turn left** downhill and **turn right** along the next track. After a wall and a gate the farm track swings away right uphill; our path continues **straight ahead** across some rougher ground before rejoining the farm track down to a gate.

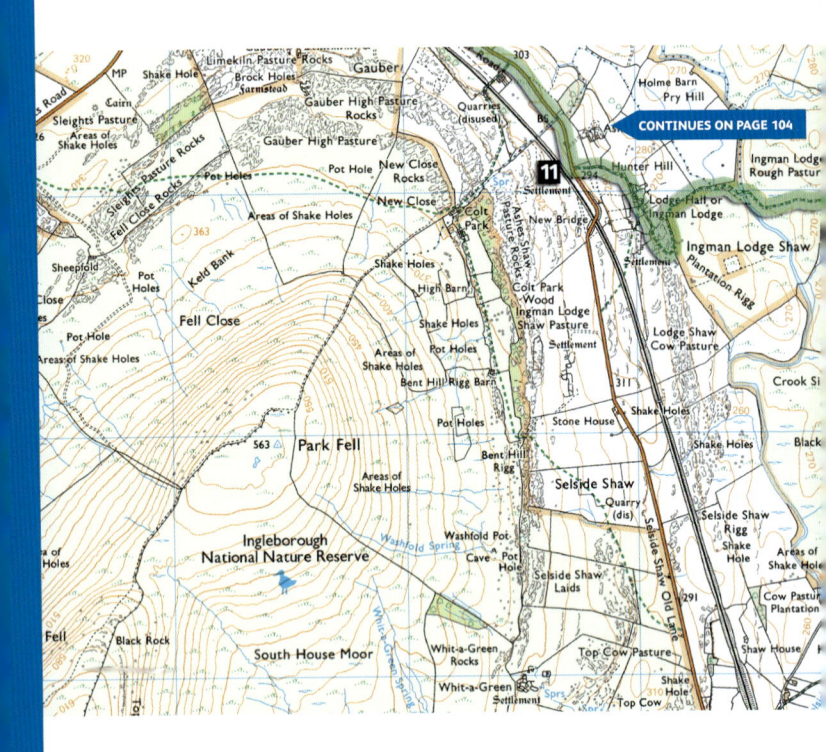

10 This is God's Bridge, a natural bridge formed by a short cave – this can be seen by peering down the riverbed to the right. It's also a good point to pick up water. Continue down the farm track to a footbridge over Ling Gill Beck on the right-hand side of the farm buildings at Nether Lodge. Through the gate **turn immediately left** and then pick up the big farm road as it comes out of the yard heading right. Follow this as it crosses rough pasture with a bridge over the infant River Ribble. After the river the track starts to climb gently and curves round to the farm at Lodge Hall. Here you join tarmac. Keep **straight ahead** uphill to a gate and cattle grid just before the main road.

11 **Turn right** and follow the road to Ribblehead. There is a bit of a path on the verge at times, at other times not. The road can get very busy, so be aware.

At Ribblehead there is parking, often a tea van, the Station Inn and the railway station. The Station Inn has kindly provided Portaloos in their car park which can be used by walkers. They ask that you contribute to the running costs by making a donation or buying something in the pub. There are also toilets inside the pub for customers. Food is served 12–9 p.m. at the time of writing.

> **Bail-out point:** you can easily be picked up from Ribblehead, or catch a train back to Settle then a bus to Ingleton.

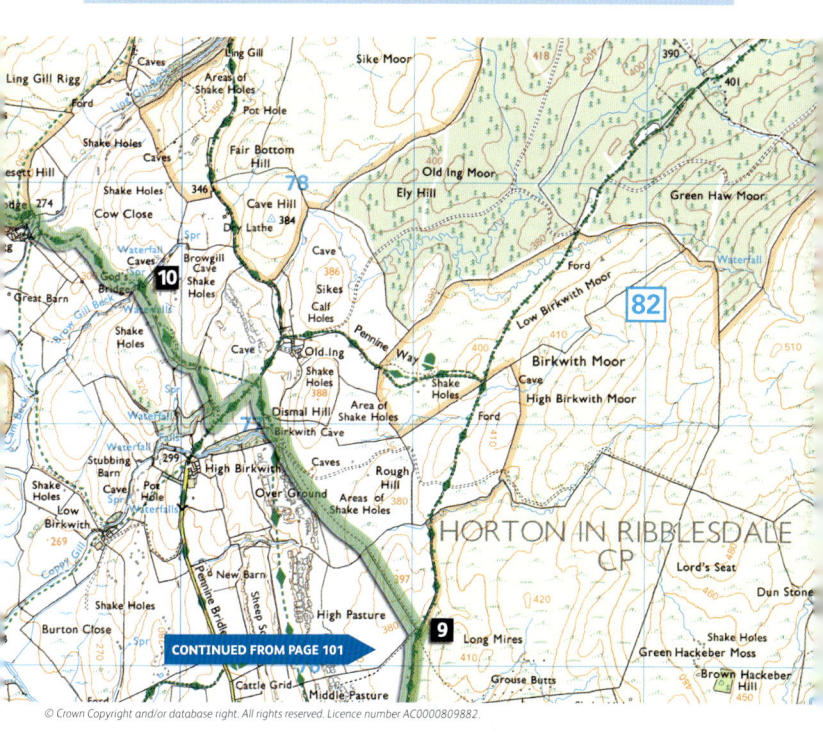

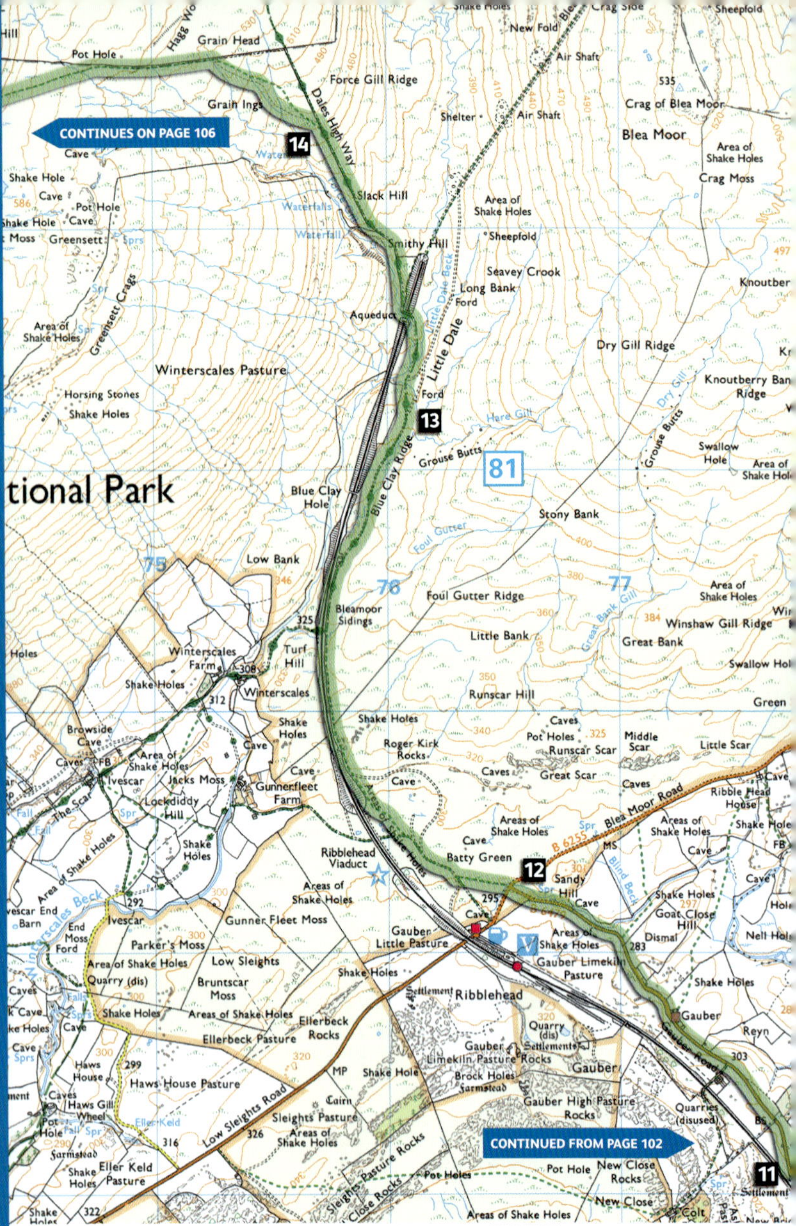

© Crown Copyright and/or database right. All rights reserved. Licence number AC0000809882.

15 / SECTION 3: RIBBLEHEAD TO INGLETON

DISTANCE 17.2KM/10.7 MILES
ASCENT 520M

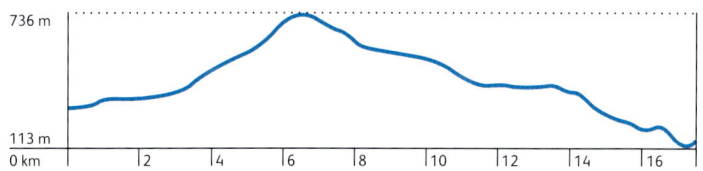

12 From the road junction take the gravelled path heading towards the viaduct. This joins a larger gravelled track. Where this larger track swings round under the viaduct, continue **straight ahead** on the smaller path heading parallel to the railway to climb a set of steps. Continue on this clear track.

13 About 600m after Blea Moor signal box there is a fork in the path (SD 760 812): **fork left** and drop down to cross the river. The path then climbs slightly to cross the railway and then starts to steepen as it climbs Slack Hill. The gradient gets a little more gentle and the old road to Dent continues straight on.

14 The path up to Whernside clearly leads off on the **left**. It's the obvious path – wider and more maintained than the old road, and signposted over the stile. It's then simply a case of following this path up and around to the left (west and then south) to the top of Whernside. There is a shelter at the top and the trig point is through the drystone wall. Third and final hill done.

15 Continue **south** on the broad path down the ridge. When the main path swings left and steeply down, instead continue **straight ahead** by the wall and follow this wall and path down the ridge. After about 5km when you have come back on to the limestone there will be a small shelter and cairn on the left; not long after these, you drop down a larger limestone bluff where the path straight on peters out – head **left** along the line of the limestone and join the broad main grassy track. Keep on the largest of the tracks as it wends down Twisleton Scar to join the track at the top of waterfalls walk.

16 **Turn left** along the track and then **right** to pick up the tarmacked road through the buildings, ignoring the signs for the waterfalls walk. Follow this down the hill to a gate where you join Oddies Lane. **Turn right** and head downhill along this quiet lane back into Ingleton. **Turn left** at the T-junction crossing the river with fine views of the viaduct on your right. **Turn right** up The Rake, keep **straight ahead/right** along Bank Top and **turn left** up the steps to the car park just before the railway bridge.

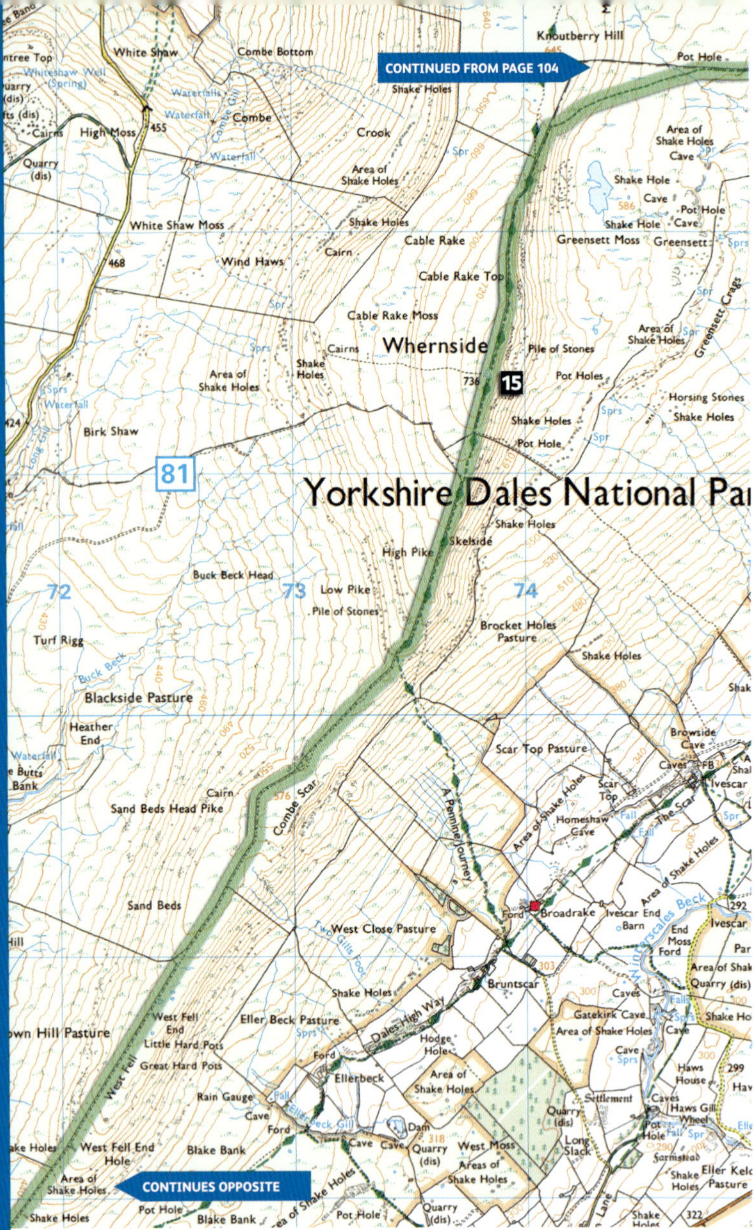
CONTINUED FROM PAGE 104
Knoutberry Hill
Pot Hole
White Shaw
Combe Bottom
Shake Holes
Waterfalls
Waterfall
Combe
High Moss
455
Quarry (dis)
Crook
Area of Shake Holes
White Shaw Moss
468
Wind Haws
Cairn
Cable Rake
Cable Rake Top
Cable Rake Moss
Greensett Moss
Greensett
Greensett Crags
Shake Hole
Cave
Whernside
Cairns
Pile of Stones
736
15
Pot Holes
Horsing Stones
Birk Shaw
Long Gill
81
Yorkshire Dales National Park
Skelside
High Pike
Buck Beck Head
Low Pike
72
73
74
Turf Rigg
Brocket Holes Pasture
Buck Beck
Blackside Pasture
Heather End
Butts Bank
Browside Cave
Caves
FB
Ivescar
Scar Top Pasture
Scar Top
Homeshaw Cave
The Scar
Sand Beds Head Pike
Combe Scar
A Pennine Journey
Area of Shake Holes
Sand Beds
Broadrake
Ford
Ivescar End
Barn
End Moss Ford
Winterscales Beck
292
West Close Pasture
Two Gills Foot
Bruntscar
303
Quarry (dis)
Gatekirk Cave
Dales High Way
Eller Beck Pasture
West Fell End
Little Hard Pots
Great Hard Pots
Hodge Hole
Ellerbeck
Haws House
299
Rain Gauge
Ellerbeck Gill
Settlement
Haws Gill Wheel
West Fell
Dam
318
West Moss
Areas of Shake Holes
Long Slack
Pot Hole
Farmstead
Eller Keld Pasture
West Fell End Hole
Blake Bank
CONTINUES OPPOSITE
Pot Hole
322

15 / THREE PEAKS FROM INGLETON   107

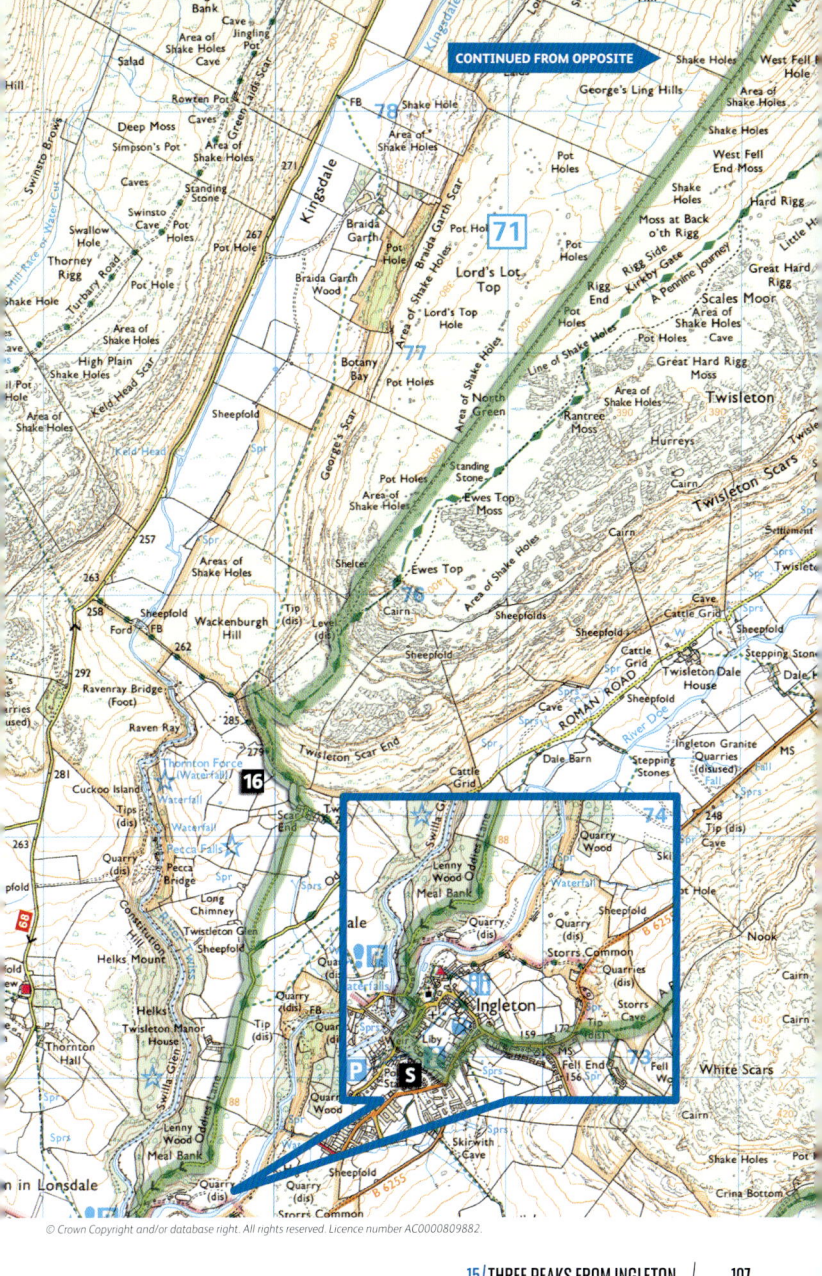

Lime kiln near Chapel-le-Dale.

/ GOOD TO KNOW

PUBLIC TRANSPORT AND ACCESS

Ingleton is connected with Kirkby Lonsdale and Settle along the A65 by the 581 Craven Connection bus which stops at the car park. The car park has toilets, a tourist information point, a community centre and a cricket pitch. There's another car park just up the road.

En route, Horton has a railway station on the Settle–Carlisle line, and bus connections (DalesBus 11) to Settle. Trains from Ribblehead run to Horton and Settle.

WHEN TO WALK IT

In terms of terrain underfoot, the whole walk is pretty weatherproof due to the maintained paths, apart from the section descending from Whernside back into Ingleton. What you really need is enough light and an early enough start. May to September has the light and hopefully the weather. Be aware that what is a blustery breeze in the valley will make walking on the tops difficult, and very tiring. Also be aware that on hot sunny days there is very little shelter anywhere on the walk. It's also wise to avoid race days: the Three Peaks cyclo-cross race is usually the last weekend in September, and the fell race the end of April.

TERRAIN AND NAVIGATION

There is a lot of ascent and descent, sometimes on steep paths and sometimes on bedrock which can be slippery. Generally, the paths are well-maintained and the bogs of the previous century covered with flagged and made paths. The route finding is generally straightforward, well signposted and easy to follow. It's still crucial to

Oddies Lane.

take the correct path off the summit of Ingleborough, and not to blindly follow the main route off Whernside; in mist and low cloud this may require a map and compass and the ability to use both.

FACILITIES AND REFRESHMENTS
Toilets in the car park. Plenty of cafes and pubs, and there's a chippy in town. There's also a Co-op.

DOGS AND KIDS
It's a very long way, and it's a very tough walk. Think carefully about whether your dog or child is going to be happy and comfortable.

POINTS OF INTEREST
This is an even longer walk than the traditional route and is likely to be much quieter on the first and last sections. Plus, you are starting with Ingleborough as your first hill, not last as is the convention, so hopefully you'll be out of step with many of the other Three Peakers on a fine day. The ascent of Ingleborough through Crina Bottom is a fascinating insight into the glacial influence on the area, both in terms of erosion and deposition.

The descent of Whernside down the full ridge is long but full of great views, plus the last section into town is on the (probable) line of Roman road 73 – the same one that comes over Cam Fell from Bainbridge. This is the probable line of the Roman road (RR73) from Bainbridge. It's now a holloway and with tired legs you'll appreciate the zigzag line the Romans built on the steeper lower section. Contrary to popular belief, the Romans did like a zigzag where necessary.

15 / THREE PEAKS FROM INGLETON

/ APPENDIX

TOURIST INFORMATION
/ *www.visityorkshire.com* – tourism information.

/ *www.yorkshiredales.org.uk* – national park website, with tourism, conservation, travel and car park information. Also has Three Peaks souvenirs and much advice about group attempts.

SELECTED PUBS, CAFES & PLACES TO STAY
There are any number of good places to eat, drink and stay near the Three Peaks. The following is just a selection. For more info, visit the websites listed above.

/ **The Old Sawmill Cafe**, Clapham
www.oldsawmillcafe.co.uk .... **T** 01524 237 788

/ **Elaine's Tea Rooms**, Feizor
www.elainestearooms.com .... **T** 01729 824 114

/ **Craven Heifer**, Stainforth
www.cravenheiferstainforth.co.uk .... **T** 01729 822 435

/ **The Marton Arms**, Thornton in Lonsdale
www.martonarms.co.uk .... **T** 01524 242 204

/ **Station Inn**, Ribblehead
www.thestationinnribblehead.com .... **T** 01524 241 274

/ **Old Hill Inn**, Chapel-le-Dale
www.oldhillinningleton.co.uk .... **T** 01524 241 256

/ **Philpin Farm Campsite**, Chapel-le-Dale
www.philpinfarm.co.uk .... **T** 01524 241 846

/ **High Laning Campsite**, Dent
www.highlaning.com .... **T** 01539 625 239

/ **Knight Stainforth Campsite**, Stainforth
www.knightstainforth.co.uk .... **T** 01729 822 200

/ **Holme Farm Campsite**, Horton .... **T** 01729 860 281

/ **YHA Ingleton**
www.yha.org.uk/hostel/yha-ingleton .... **T** 0345 260 2752

/ **YHA Malham**
www.yha.org.uk/hostel/yha-malham .... **T** 0345 371 9529

PUBLIC TRANSPORT
TRAINS
| *www.nationalrail.co.uk*

Settle–Carlisle Railway: for our purposes, this connects Settle with Horton and Ribblehead.

Settle is connected to Leeds on the main railway network.

Clapham station is connected to Lancaster from the west. If you wanted to get to Settle from the west, you would need to either go via Leeds or go to Long Preston and change to catch a train back to Settle. If you are interested, it's fascinating (if frustrating) to look at the history of the railway connection to Ingleton, now long gone.

BUSES
The number 11 DalesBus rus runs from Settle to Horton, but no further up the valley.
www.dalesbus.org

The number 581 Craven Connection bus goes from Settle up the A65 to Ingleton and Clapham and back. ***www.klch.co.uk/bus-services***

There is a really random and not very useful seasonal service from Kirkby Lonsdale to Hawes via Ribblehead. The Arriva 832 runs on a Sunday and Bank Holidays, once in either direction. It stops at both Ribblehead and the Old Hill Inn. ***www.dalesbus.org***

TAXIS
| **Bentham Taxis** .... **T** 07768 571 407
| **Austwick Taxis** .... **T** 01524 251 364
| **Settle Taxis** .... **T** 01729 824 824

GEAR SHOPS
| **Inglesport**, Ingleton
  www.inglesport.com

| **Castleberg Outdoors**, Settle
  www.castlebergoutdoors.co.uk

| **Cotswold Outdoor**, Skipton
  www.cotswoldoutdoor.com

MOUNTAIN WEATHER
Both the Mountain Weather Information Service and Met Office provide dedicated mountain forecasts for the Yorkshire Dales National Park and the Three Peaks.
| *www.mwis.org.uk*
| *www.metoffice.gov.uk* – including forecasts for all three summits

SHOW CAVES
| **Ingleborough Cave**
  www.ingleboroughcave.co.uk

| **White Scar Cave**
  www.whitescarcave.co.uk

Climbing Ingleborough from the Chapel-le-Dale side, Whernside and Ribblehead in the distance. © Stephen Ross

SWIMMING SPOTS
| **Catrigg Force**, Stainforth SD 831 671
| **Stainforth Force**, Stainforth SD 818 671

CHEESE
One of the best cheese shops in the country is on the A65.
| **The Courtyard Dairy**
  www.thecourtyarddairy.co.uk

USEFUL WEBSITES
| *www.dalesrocks.org.uk* – geology and more
| *www.adventuresmart.uk* – general planning and safety information
| *www.3peakscyclocross.org.uk* – website for the annual cyclo-cross race
| *www.threepeaksrace.org* – website for the annual fell race
| *www.settle-carlisle.co.uk* – the Settle–Carlisle Railway Development Company, a not-for-profit limited company since 1992

REFERENCES
| ***Day Walks in the Yorkshire Dales***
  Bernard Newman, Vertebrate Publishing
| ***Pennine Bridleway***
  Hannah Collingridge, Vertebrate Publishing
| ***The Yorkshire Dales: Landscape and geology***
  Tony Waltham, The Crowood Press

ABOUT THE AUTHOR

Hannah Collingridge is a freelance writer, and keen hillwalker and mountain biker. She's fascinated by landscape and geomorphology, rocks, place names and just generally being somewhere interesting poking at things. She's walked, ridden, explored and played in the Dales for over 40 years. Her work has appeared in *Cranked*, *Cycle* and *Singletrack* magazines, and she is the author of *Pennine Bridleway*. She is happiest when pointing excitedly at something, which is just before the arm-waving stage. Mostly fuelled by cheese and coffee.

VERTEBRATE PUBLISHING
MOUNTAIN WALKS

15 inspiring walks with summit routes and lower-level alternatives for mixed weather or shorter days and those new to mountain walking

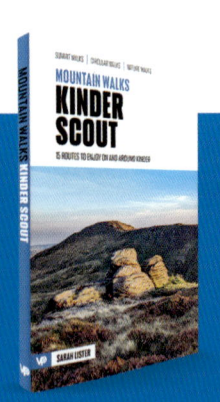

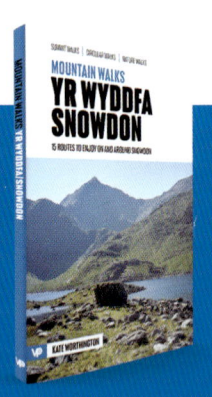

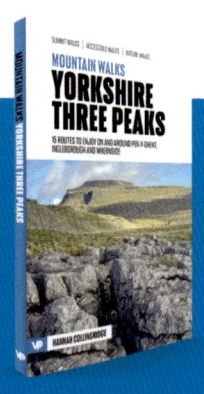

- Stunning photography
- **Ordnance Survey** 1:25,000 maps
- Downloadable GPX files
- Easy-to-follow, detailed directions
- Essential public transport, safety and navigation advice

Available from outdoor shops, bookshops and direct
www.adventurebooks.com

inspiring adventure